# BEFORE THE DREADFUL DAYLIGHT STARTS

*An Anthology of Norfolk Poetry*

Edited by
Cameron Self and Kevin Gardner
Introduction by Jeremy Noel-Tod

WATERLAND BOOKS

Front cover photograph of Hunstanton: Stephen Hyatt-Cross
Back cover drawing: Brograve Mill by Tom Grayling
Back cover haiku: Cameron Self
Design/typesetting: Nick Stone
Second Edition October 2023
Published by Waterland Books, 2023
ISBN: 978-1-7396034-2-7
Waterland Books, Norwich, Norfolk
Printed in Great Britain

*For Nicki and Hilary*

# CONTENTS

## From Homer to Cromer: The Poetry of Norfolk

For many people, coming and going on holiday, the Norfolk coast, which rounds out the east of England with a lobe of eroding land, is the only part of the county they ever really get to know – and even then they will be looking away, out to sea. More of Norfolk's border is exposed to the ocean than not, and this makes for a mood of collective isolation; an open loneliness intensified by the fact that no motorway has yet crossed its land border. 'How did the Devil come? When first attack?' asks John Betjeman of innocent childhood holidays in Norfolk, and the obvious answer is: over the North Sea, with the cold wind and the snow buntings.

Poets, too, have flocked to the edges, for cliffs, dunes and saltmarshes, and that is where this book begins. But the poetry of the Norfolk coast is almost entirely a modern invention, arriving with the railways, expanding with the car. For the editors of this anthology – by far the most comprehensive and knowledgeable ever compiled – it is just a landing place: deep Norfolk lies beyond, along the waterways that lead to its boat-stirred Broads; its straggly villages and by-passed towns; its flint-walled city, Norwich, with its thin cathedral and compact castle; its grand churches – the stone legacy of the wool trade – rising above the fields; the wet Fens to the west and the dry Brecks to the south, both landscapes changed enormously by human settlement, despite the fact that there often seems to be nobody around. (All those people you can't see, however, made the rhymes attributed here to 'Anon'.)

When Edward Lear composed his limerick about the Old Person of Cromer who stood on one leg to read Homer, it was probably the first time in the history of English literature that the fishing town – and fashionable Victorian resort – had been rhymed with the Greek epic poet. John Taylor, at least, didn't think to make the connection when he recounted being washed up there in 1622, despite casting himself as a hapless Odysseus, sucked into the whirlpool of Charybdis. But as Homer's ghost whispered to the Irish poet Patrick Kavanagh, in a sonnet ironically titled 'Epic': 'I made the *Iliad* from such / A local row'.

Modern poetry has specialised in making something out of nothing – and there is plenty of nothing in Norfolk, from the ruins of its great houses to the 'ghost fields' left behind by the U.S. Air Force after the war. One of my favourite sections of the local paper is the farming news, which often features pictures of nothing: blocks, that is, of 'productive arable land', for sale by auction. 'The inner spirit of the world', wrote the poet T.E. Hulme, 'is miles and miles of ploughed fields'. A poem puts the human imagination back into this speechless space, like Tariq in Moniza Alvi's 'Rural Scene', who moves under 'luminous Norfolk skies /... / as if he is walking a tiger'. Welcome.

*Jeremy Noel-Tod*

# COAST

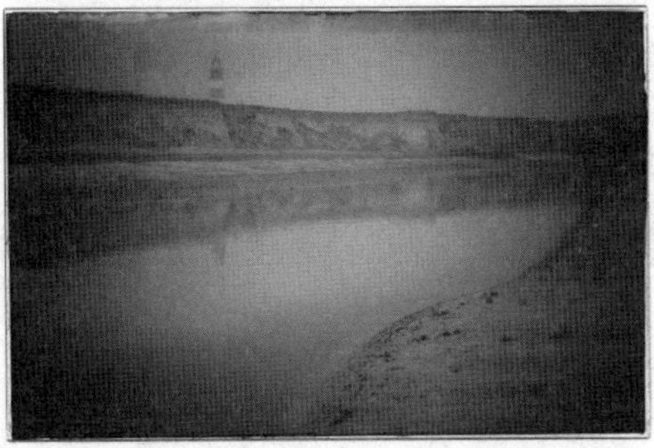

## Salthouse

When we walked up the hill above Salthouse
and saw, looking down where we'd been

ourselves on the beach waving back –
we were here and there and no-place

coming and going at once, perceiving
the speckled clouds as sleeping seals,

as we dipped our toes in the breeze
and watched from the hill's shoreline

a kestrel come in with the tide,
and hold his stillness open

over the ship weathervane
of a church that was floating and drowned,

his shadow on the ground beneath him
the anchor that kept him aloft.

*Charles Bennett (1954-*

## Ghazal: Cley

Gentled in the blue-black broth, vanishing circles of Cley.
A returning song, migration song living in the mouth of Cley.

Surrender here, your eyes, ears, scratch out a song
A double tongued subsong, carried in the eggs of Cley.

The young crouch, the reed draws out the moths.
Shadow paints shadow into the silence of Cley.

Bird wired to breath, unveil, draw a line, a thread.
Swift things . . . vanishings, eye, the returning song of Cley.

*Mona Arshi (1970-*

## Snettisham

This is the Wash it seems –
a last exhalation
of the dying land, or something
the sea's been working on
for ages: sketching it in,
rubbing it out,
redoing and redoing it,
never satisfied.

Look at you, all wrapped up,
hat and scarf and
gloves, and those wild eyes
made weak by medication
and hopes confounded so
so many times.
Never this thin before.
Going slowly, in this
flattest part of England,
going slowly downhill.

The birds rise
like a handful of rain
thrown upward,

and the Great Twitcher
in the sky misses
nothing. His fondness
for sparrows is well known.

*David Callin (1958-*

## Sunrise on Brancaster Beach

Bent with gentle heaviness, the old,
bald head of earth, explained in yellow light,
gets licked to life again. The sea looks white,
like bitten skin; the wrinkled sand feels cold.
This is the end of night: and from its sleep,
whose sweet corruption burns me like a match
just struck, the world is laboured out. A patch
of orange cloud turns pale. I shiver. Deep,
deep beyond the air where words, ideas
and minds are kept convinced, I only see
the churning of great planets – one with me,
the rest without. I yawn. The sun appears
and all the earth is warm. And even I
applaud, with half a smile the bloodless sky.

*John Gallas (1950-*

## A Very Merry Wherry-Ferry-Voyage

And thus half soused, half stewed, with sea and sweat,
We land at Cromer Town half dry, half wet;
But we supposing all was safe and well,
In shunning Scylla on Charybdis fell;
For why, some women and some children there
That saw us land, were all possessed with fear;
And much amaz'd ran crying up and down,
That enemies were come to take the town.
Some said that we were pirates, some said thieves,
And what the women says, the men believes.
With that four constables did quickly call,
Your aid! To arms your men of Cromer all.
Then straightway forty men with rusty bills,
Some arm'd in ale, all of approved skill,
Divided into four stout regiments,
To guard the city from dangerous events.
Brave Captain Pescod did the vanguard lead,
And Captain Clarke the rearward governed,
Whilst Captain Wiseman and hot Captain Kimble,
Were in main battalia fierce and nimble.

... Some rascals ran into my boat apace,
And turn'd and tumbled her, like men of Gotham,
Quite topsy-turvy upward with her bottom,
Vowing they would in tatters piece-meal tear
They cursed pirate's boat, that bred their fear;
And I am sure, their madness (to my harm)
Tore a board out much longer than mine arm.
And they so bruis'd and split our wherry, that
She leaked, we cast out water with a hat.
Now let men judge, upon this truth revealing,
If Turks or Moors could use more barb'rous dealing;
Or whether it be fit I should not write,
Their envy, foolish fear, and mad despite.
What may wise men conceive, when they shall note,
That five unarmed men in a wherry boat,
Naught to defend, or to offend with stripes,
But one old sword and two tobacco pipes;
And that of constables a murnivall,
Men, women, children, all in general,
And that they all should be so valiant wise,
To fear we would a market town surprise.

... Sweet Mr. Pescod's double diligence,
Had horsed himself to bear intelligence
To justices of peace within the land,
What dangerous business there was now at hand.
There was I forced to tarry all the while,
Till some said he rode four-and-twenty mile,
In seeking men of worship, peace, and quorum,
Most wisely to declare strange news before um.
And whatsoever tales he did recite,
I sure he caused Sir Austin Palgrave, knight,
And Mr. Robert Kemp, a justice there,
Came before me to know how matters were.
As conference 'twixt them and I did pass,
They quickly understood me what I was;
And though they knew me not in prose and looks,
They had read of me in my verse and books.
My business's account I there did make,
And I and all my company did take
The lawful oath of our allegiance then,
By which we were believed for honest men.

... Besides, Sir Austin Palgrave bade me this,
To go but four miles, where his dwelling is,
And I and all my company should there
Find friendly welcome, mixed with other cheer.
I gave them thanks, and so I'll give them still,
And did accept their cheer in their good will.
Then 3 o'clock at afternoon and past,
I was discharged from Cromer at the last.
But for men should not think that enviously
Against this town I let my lines to fly;
And that I do not lie, or scoff, or fable,
For then I will write something charitable.
It is an ancient market town that stands
Upon a lofty cliff of mouldring sands;
The sea against the cliffs doth daily beat,
And every tide into the land doth eat.
The town is poor, unable by expense,
Against the raging sea to make defence;
And every day it eateth further in,
Still waiting, washing down the sand doth win,
That if some course be not ta'en speedily,
The town's in danger in the sea to lie.
A goodly church stands on these brittle grounds,

Not many fairer in Great Britain's bounds;
And if the sea shall swallow it as some fear,
'Tis not ten thousand pounds the like could rear.
No Christian can behold it but with grief,
And with my heart I wish them quick relief.
So farewell, Cromer, I have spoke for thee,
Though you did'st much unkindly deal with me...

*John Taylor (1578-1653)*

## Sea Wall, Overy Staithe

Running I become
the bank's long legs
and bendy knees
Sometimes I outwit time
a quickening into the moment
knowing every step
will take me somewhere
different

Travellers with tripods
picnics  rucksacks  guns
worm-diggers
the cyclists and the day trippers
have met my several selves –
patterns of early footprints
loosing energy into the dunes
where space opens

Vermuyden's men
with weather-beaten faces
first held in the sea
and now again
a team
strip back to bones
the mallows clover chamomile
while the driver
high on caterpillar tracks
slaps and spreads clay emulsion

I am the length and breadth
of what's unchanged
am lapwing (disappearing)
butterflies in spiral
acrobat (my shadow)
natterjack (my song)
windslam across the saltings
beneath enormous skies

Voices are silent
Trees that bore the dog rose
and the tiny self-sown apples
Gone
Still I run
look backwards and look forwards

Allow this poem
to carry you beyond

*Sally Festing (1938-*

## Salthouse, Norfolk

Even on midsummer days a spongy mist
Swirls round the marshes and the sun is subdued.
The sluggish grey sea's thud and the stark flint church
Emphasize the silence and the solitude.

It may be human fantasy that lends
An aspect of desolation to this village.
We are saddened to reflect that sullen tides,
Lashed from somnolence, will rise and pillage

The hoarded treasure of these fishermen
Who stubbornly breed their pigs and ducks and cows,
Knowing a score of years the longest respite
The whim of Nature contemptuously allows.

Perhaps if we came here with unburdened hearts
The marram grass and salt marsh would assume
The savour and the promise of ripening corn
And the sea would flash with iridescent spume.

But I believe that some original taint
Haunts and infects with foreboding the heavy skies,
Benumbing the flints and beasts and earth with grief
Which we do not invent but recognise.

*John Press (1920-2007)*

## Boulders on Hunstanton Beach

Because all cockling, musselling and oystering rights here
belong, as they do, to a certain leStrange –
which right is described by a sign and a boundary line –
all along the beach and pale view from half a pier
your doggy exercise, hoovering for a spjót or páll,
bright bird binoculars and small digestive walks, all
are honest acts, unmuddied by some ebb and flow
of secret intent, not done-but-not-meant
by obsequious travellers here below.

This low tide there's a tractor up to its floor in sea
pretending to be some enthusiast or other about the view,
dipping a silver trailer in forbidden grounds
half a mile out in the wind for something –
something fishy: but nothing new.
No burble or glitter of disguise confounds
a well-run Deity.

Witness punishment: for their old
cockle-dreams, mussel-ruts and
oyster-itch both large and small,
regard this hellish fall!

One thousand buried transgressors!
Oh, they might look like boulders to you;
no, no, even to you they are skulls,
wigged in greenweed, confined
for enterprises of a private kind.

Moon-struck tides pay their respects
and bow away again,
this courtesy one happy effect
of the alarmless measure of things
by which we get a flake of light:
but whether this colloidal hiss
brings up more sand upon their heads
than it takes, ebbing, away,
is a matter more of morals than of motion.

Obsessively this grey sheet is drawn
across their beds that is their second night
and as often uncovered. Where is the sense in that?

This morning one more dome is sludged?
Start hammering your arks together!
God's second, cross noyade starts here:
but tomorrow the top of one white ear
just like a shell appears – again –
ah, and we are discovered, pardoned,
and wait for an excellent rainbow,
forgiving weather, and the end of rain.

How ravelled a moral universe is
while Justice grows, falters, fails and reverses
and divine anger gathers and disperses.

If leStrange were God it would be odd
to prefer such tangled East-Anglian winds
of how and why
to the sky,
a favourite of painters here
for its unobstructed arch and brilliant blue,
its empty, motionless, notionless curlicue.

*John Gallas (1950-*

## Thoughts at Happisburgh

Remember the long combes tunnelling into summer
Cumulus tossed into towers and keeps above,
The trampled cliff paths sweet with gorse and bracken
Around each known, each named, particular cove,
And by this touchstone from the years of promise
Happisburgh cracks in dry impersonal pieces –
The reeds, the marram grass, a north wind whipping
The anonymous flat sea margins, the huts, some caravans,
And over it all the sky enormously drifting
In endless thin layers of cloud: undesired
Featureless landscape where the intruding figures
Loom up too large and loud.

At first when sea meant only the brown flood
Of Bristol Channel, the flats of opal mud
Whitened with dizzying gulls when neap tides came,
Rough dogs, wild tumbling boys, far bathers' cries
And sheltered ladies safe to ask the time –
Through the diminishing glass of childish eyes
The shore was all and only wind and sun
And furious scrunch of sand on wooden spades,
Around the lighthouse bunkered in the dunes
No footsteps save one's own.

Later – in a numinous hour – the lapis bay,
The scent of briar and garlic from lush inland lanes
Blown seaward, the rock pools drinking up the Atlantic sky,
The halcyon daylight sucked down into caves –
Then it was we, not I (but it was plural I),
Sharing the timeless spiral of a day
That was all of light and water, air and fire;
And far below though still on the same shore
The rest were only lilliputian men
Speaking a stranger's language yet unknown:

Learning it is the hard thing. Happisburgh is a teacher
Pounding the grammar, rewarding with a poem:
For here beyond the caravans a village grows
In farms and elms and sheep-pens and a vigilant tower
Where Happisburgh church that great ark of light
Is filled with years of prayers, of griefs and fears
And homeliness, loving memorials no less
Of Kosikot and Cartref than of these generations
Whose tombstone lockers lie awash in grass;
For this is a father's house where children come
And share their equalness: sameness not difference is the stem
For uncounted variations. And each is known by name.

*Joan Barton (1908-1986)*

## The Sea, The Sea

In a house
at the edge of a cliff
you can hear the sea
even with the windows closed
but at night
in your small bedroom
with the green and brown leaves
rustling the wallpaper
you leave the window open
to the wind
and even in your sleep
hear the sea slap and suck
and the pebbles running back
to where they were made

but the edge of the world
is crumbling
and houses with both closed and open windows
fall into the sea
with shops and churches
which according to legend
still sound their bells in storms

and in those smug houses
which are safe from erosion
the sea
even with its windows open
and the wind at its back
whispers so far away
it is lost in the conversation of dreams

until now
with so little time left
almost any empty house will do
near or far from the sea
even if you have to change the wallpaper.

*Edwin Brock (1927-1997)*

## Hopton-on-Sea

When I can clearly see the stars,
I aim, true as a laser beam, into space
and rebound, a child in your arms

shirking sleep, confident that I will be carried
from the Silver Dollar cabaret
to the cradle of the caravan.

The smell of the gas cooker warms us
more than its see-through blue. We sit on our beds
to eat. Prawn cocktail crisps and card games

punctuate the rain. The salt of sea and crackers
coats my lips like doughnut sugar. The sand
works my skin, smoothing, smoothing.

The chevronned, stainless steel steps,
removable, lead my jelly shoes to a world
of bare open skies.

*Heidi Williamson (1971-*

## Here, at the Tide's Turning

You close your eyes and see

  the stillness of
the mullet-nibbled arteries, samphire
on the mudflats almost underwater,
and on the saltmarsh whiskers of couch-grass
twitching, waders roosting, sea-lavender
faded to ashes.

  In the dark or almost dark
shapes sit on the staithe muttering of plickplack,
and greenshanks, and zos beds;

  a duck arrives
in a flap, late for a small pond party.

The small yard's creak and groan and lazy rap,
muffled water-music.

  One sky-streamer,
pale and half-frayed, still dreaming of colour.

Water and earth and air quite integral:
all Waterslain one sombre aquarelle.

From the beginning, and last year, this year,
you can think of no year when you have
not sat on this stub of a salt-eaten stanchion.

Dumbfounded by such tracts of marsh and sky –
the void swirled round you and pressed against you –
you've found a mercy in small stones.

This year, next year, you cannot think
of not returning: not to perch in the blue
hour on this blunt jetty, not to wait, as of right,
for the iron hour and the turning of the tide.

You cross the shillying and the shallows
and, stepping on to the marsh, enter
a wilderness.

   Quick wind works around you.

You are engulfed in a wave of blue flames.

No line that is not clear cut and severe,
nothing baroque or bogus. The voices
of young children rehearsing on the staithe
are lifted from another time.

   This is
battleground. Dark tide fills the winking pulks,
floods the mud-canyons.

   This flux, this anchorage.

Here you watch, you write, you tell the tides.

   You walk clean into the possible.

*Kevin Crossley-Holland (1941-*

## The Mill Garden

Stately stand the sunflowers, glowing down the garden-side,
Ranged in royal rank arow along the warm grey wall,
Whence their deep disks burn at rich midnoon afire with pride,
Even as though their beams indeed were sunbeams, and the tall
Sceptral stems bore stars whose reign endures, not flowers that fall.
Lowlier laughs and basks the kindlier flower of homelier fame,
Held by love the sweeter that it blooms in Shakespeare's name,
Fragrant yet as though his hand had touched and made it thrill,
Like the whole world's heart, with warm new life and gladdening flame.
Fair befall the fair green close that lies below the mill!

Softlier here the flower-soft feet of refluent seasons glide,
Lightlier breathes the long low note of change's gentler call.
Wind and storm and landslip feed the lone sea's gulf outside,
Half a seamew's first flight hence; but scarce may these appal
Peace, whose perfect seal is set for signet here on all.
Steep and deep and sterile, under fields no plough can tame,
Dip the cliffs full-fledged with poppies red as love or shame,
Wide wan daisies bleak and bold, or herbage harsh and chill;
Here the full clove pinks and wallflowers crown the love they claim.
Fair befall the fair green close that lies below the mill!

All the place breathes low, but not for fear lest ill betide,
Soft as roses answering roses, or a dove's recall.
Little heeds it how the seaward banks may stoop and slide,
How the winds and years may hold all outer things in thrall,
How their wrath may work on hoar church tower and boundary wall.
Far and wide the waste and ravin of their rule proclaim
Change alone the changeless lord of things, alone the same:
Here a flower is stronger than the winds that work their will,
Or the years that wing their way through darkness toward their aim.
Fair befall the fair green close that lies below the mill!

Friend, the home that smiled us welcome hither when we came,
When we pass again with summer, surely should reclaim
Somewhat given of heart's thanksgiving more than words fulfil –
More than song, were song more sweet than all but love, might frame.
Fair befall the fair green close that lies below the mill!

*A.C. Swinburne (1837-1909)*

## Morston Marshes

Into this muddy coastline
the North Sea seeps silently
twice a day
under the kestrel's weather eye
in the growing puddles
gulls drill the marsh
for nothing we can see
or screech their territory
like fishwives
from the tops of poles

even in August
the sky drowns us
in small drops
settling on hair and eyes
wanting us flying in it
or grovelling in the ooze
at the water's edge

I died in this country
and came back
to pay my debts
to its wetlands

something fishes me
all the way
back to where it began

and is beginning again
down the years

with a million denials.

*Edwin Brock (1927-1997)*

## Walking with a Poet at Burnham Overy Staithe

I.

My shadow floats alongside me, cut crisp
as paper from sheets of light.

Water bubbles, burbles in the channel.
A boat chug-chugs past with a black dog
at its prow, attentive.

Spectacles full of marsh tide,
you hold up your notebook
to the blue pupil of the iPad lens

which captures pen marks that are threads, scraps
not yet sewn into lines.

We sit on a bench
knocked off its even keel by the roar of the wind that can
rush in from the pale gold North,
with Alexander seed pods rattling beside our ears.

Not speaking, we lean our faces
into the salty maw of the sea-god
feeling the first hints of the lull, the torpor that will follow.

2.

An egret stalks the water meadows on black-stilt legs
with steps that barely stir the water.

Dart of black beak. Swallow small silver wriggle.

A spoonbill dredges a pond where cygnets sail
protected by the prowl of pen and swan.

A smatter of ducks.
The hush hush hush of the reed beds.

We lag, dawdle,
passing words between us.

*Caroline Gilfillan (1951-*

## Eccles

Cliffs sifting down, stiff grassblades bent,
Subdued, and shouldering off thick sand,
Boulders – compacted grout and flint –
Jut from a stranded beach, a land
Adhering lightly to the sea.
Tide-drenched, withdrawn, and drowned again,
Capsized, these buttresses still strain
Towards perpendicularity.

The place-name mimes the fallen church,
Abbreviated, shrunk to this
Truncated word, echo of speech,
A Latin ghost's thin obsequies
Carried by wind, answered by sea –
Ecclesia: the syllables
Curtailed, half heard, like tongueless bells
From empty steeples endlessly.

*Anthony Thwaite (1930-2021)*

## Happisburgh Haiku

This is the crumbling
Edge – where the land surrenders
Itself to the sea.

Everything here is
Impermanent – everything
Here is eternal.

You are soft; you are
Sea-bitten; you are waiting;
You are Happisburgh.

The land is fragile;
The land is failing; and your
Time is running out.

This long parish: long
Defended; long attacked; long
Settled. Not long left.

For centuries you
Have stood here on this hill – but
For how much longer?

*Cameron Self (1962-*

## Parking at Winterton

The roped-off drop to tufty marram
sand & the bleating body bags of seals

I sing the hundred metres of beach
car park sheared off in a spring tide

dune & asphalt                    beach café
tarred huts where I imagine

the fleeced weekenders of the soul
squatting over poured concrete

strained longshore through castellated
sea defences where I wade out

in all seasons toward however many
bathing days are left to us

& the deft shadows of the seals
                                        grey & common

who have found their forms
in the still rising water

*Matt Haw (1988-*

## Whincover

Winter's path is bramble-whipped: a scaffold
Of brittle hawthorn, dry lines of reed,
Oily dykes and yellow rinds of fields.
An unmaking yet a distillation.
A cold clearing in the dying light
When all the world seems fixed on Overy Bank;
An axis for the alabaster skies,
The breaking seas, the white knuckle dunes,
The twitching marsh's olive crackle glaze,
The haphazard houses on Overy Staithe,
The stumps of ghostly fences stretching out
To salt-washed creeks and samphire scrub.
It is a patterning that revives
The flickering needle of buried lives.

*John Golding (1965-*

## The Old Sweet Dove of Wiveton

'Twas the voice of the sweet dove
I heard him move
I heard him cry
Love, love.

High in the chestnut tree
In the nest of the old dove
And there he sits solitary
Crying, Love, love.

The gray of this heavy day
Makes the green of the trees' leaves and the grass brighter
And the flowers of the chestnut tree whiter
And whiter the flowers of the cow-parsley.
So still is the air
So heavy the sky
You can hear the splash
Of the water falling from the green grass
As Red and Honey push by,
The old dogs,
Gone away, gone hunting by the marsh bogs.

Happy the retriever dogs in their pursuit
Happy in bog-mud the busy foot.

Now all is silent, it is silent again
In the sombre day and the beginning soft rain
It is silence made more actual
By the moan from the high tree that is occasional,

Where in his nest above
Still sits the old dove,
Murmuring solitary
Crying for pain,
Crying most melancholy
Again and again.

*Stevie Smith (1902-1971)*

## On a Friend's Escape from Drowning off the Norfolk Coast

Came up that cold sea at Cromer like a running grave
   Beside him as he struck
Wildly towards the shore, but the blackcapped wave
   Crossed him and swung him back,
And he saw his son digging in the castled dirt that could save.
   Then the farewell rock
Rose a last time to his eyes. As he cried out
   A pawing gag of the sea
Smothered his cry and he sank in his own shout
   Like a dying airman. Then she
Deep near her son asleep on the hourglass sand
   Was awakened by whom
Save the Fate who knew that this was the wrong time:
   And opened her eyes
On the death of her son's begetter. Up she flies
   Into the hydra-headed
Grave as he closes his life upon her who for
   Life has so richly bedded him.
But she drove through his drowning like Orpheus and tore
   Back by the hair
Her escaping bridegroom. And on the sand their son
   Stood laughing where
He was almost an orphan. Then the three lay down
   On that cold sand,
Each holding the other by a living hand.

*George Barker (1913-1991)*

## To Paint a Salt Marsh

Samphire and mare's tail and the salt marsh.

Nothing appears to have movement here
but the birds – it is where the white tern
pivots his swift course and on the tideline
dunlin and sandpiper dibble.
                                        Otherwise,
at low tide, it's as if the brown sea
clogged in the mudflats. A spar,
tall and near the vertical, splits the view.

And on the horizon a grass-thatched sand-dune
looms like a northern fell. It
lays on the water's stillness precisely
its own stillness.

*Clive Wilmer (1945-*

## The Coast: Norfolk

As on the highway's quiet edge
He mows the grass beside the hedge,
The old man has for company
The distant, grey, salt-smelling sea,
A poppied field, a cow and calf,
The finches on the telegraph.

Across his faded back a hone,
He slowly, slowly scythes alone
In silence of the wind-soft air,
With ladies' bedstraw everywhere,
With whitened corn, and tarry poles,
And far-off gulls like risen souls.

*Frances Cornford (1886-1960)*

# BROADS & RIVERS

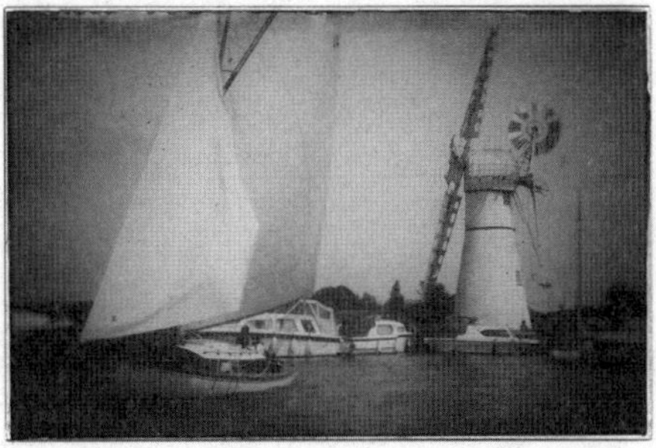

## Yare Song

Marsh lover, mud flipper
down amongst the groundlings,
moorhens, blue-lights,
sweet-shallow-mornings.

I am scaled and slithered:
strings of weed for hair,
dipping my shade-fingers
among bubbles and eddies,

spark-netted on the meanderings
of the mind's own river,
hearing the shadow-ghosts
of all those drowned girls: witches,

dipped down deep among
the slippery tendrils,
swan-necked lovelies
warbling in the reeds, singing.

*Julia Webb (1966-*

## Broadland

Only Bill's boatyard was renting; the others were close-shuttered
but a necklace of bobbing day launches flanked both sides of one pier.

The season was ending and so were we. We were over,
though habit pulled us near, on the grebe-sprinkled water,

where swans tucked their heads in behind, nudging up to the rushes,
and made do for words we couldn't know we would utter.

*Rory Waterman (1981-*

## Norfolk

How did the Devil come? When first attack?
  These Norfolk lanes recall lost innocence,
The years fall off and find me walking back
  Dragging a stick along the wooden fence
Down this same path, where, forty years ago,
My father strolled behind me, calm and slow.

I used to fill my hands with sorrel seeds
  And shower him with them from the tops of the stiles,
I used to butt my head into his tweeds
  To make him hurry down those languorous miles
Of ash and alder-shaded lanes, till here
Our moorings and the masthead would appear.

There after supper lit by lantern light
  Warm in the cabin I could lie secure
And hear against the polished sides at night
  The lap lap lapping of the weedy Bure,
A whispering and watery Norfolk sound
Telling of all the moonlit reeds around.

How did the Devil come? When first attack?
  The church is just the same, though now I know
Fowler of Louth restored it. Time, bring back
  The rapturous ignorance of long ago,
The peace, before the dreadful daylight starts,
Of unkept promises and broken hearts.

*John Betjeman (1906-1984)*

When the sea comes in at Horsey Gap
Without any previous warning,
A swan shall build its rushy nest
On the roof of The Swan at Horning.
And a bald-headed crow, contented and merry,
Shall feast on the corpses that float by the ferry.

*Anon*

## Saturday at Wroxham

So many boats upon the river!
So many pennants all a-quiver!
So many yachts about the quays,
So many sails amongst the trees;
So many people everywhere,
So much holiday in the air!
The half-past one from Liverpool Street
So filled up to the very last seat,
And people pour out of the station
Filled with holiday jubilation:
Hurrah! Hurrah! We're here! We're here!
Luggage, luggage, everywhere –
So many come with one accord,
So many innocents abroad!
Take my luggage down to Presses' –
Do you know what Bunn's address is? –
What time do the buses go –
How can I find Brimbelow?
Hurry! Hurry! Lose no tricet
Time is flying, we may miss it!
Thus they treat with Time the fawner,
And congregate upon Roy's Corner.

I want provisions for a cruise!
I want some tins of Heinz's stews!
I want some bacon – want some bread –
No, I'll take crispbread instead.
Where do I get paraffin?
Cut the ham up nice and thin!
Can I buy fishing tackle here?
Will you supply a case of beer?
Behold the crowd around the bars,
In sweaters, shorts and panamas!
What gaiety! What summer dresses!
What damsels, in what new distresses!
Stop Me, buy one, two or three,
Strawberry for you, vanilla for me;
Let's buy sun-glasses and a map,
A guide book, and a yachting cap,
Sunburn-lotion, films, and camera,
What glorious impedimenta!
Down to the Boatyards, and the Boat,
We'll eat our first meal here afloat!

The river's packed from dusk till dawning,
From Wroxham Bridge right down to Horning.
The sails are set, the wind is wanting,
Right, you lubbers! Start off quanting!
Ah, but there's wind on Wroxham Broad;
Aye, and there's traffic. What a horde!
There's no right side and no wrong side,
Just a weak side and a strong side;
Plough down dinghies when you're merry,
But always give way to a wherry;
Gently, gently, with the paint
You might think it's tough. It ain't!
Remember, if you wouldn't bruise her,
That there's no brakes aboard a cruiser,
And if the worst comes, in your durance
Thank your stars that there's insurance.
The wise man spends his afternoon
On Wroxham Broad, for he knows soon
The breeze will drop, and leave his mast sick
At Salhouse, or at Woodbastwick.

But what a change on Sunday morning!
Everybody's gone to Horning.

*Alan Hunter (1922-2005)*

## Gale Force

With rumbling brilliant barrow-loads devise
Temple and tower of cloud upon the sky,
Let the brave arch, the column fall and rise
With engrossed genius of your slavery.

My hill is strung with your vast breath and strain,
Coils of elation tumble down to earth,
Green fills the mullions of a phantom rain,
Eternal lightning heaves and travels forth.

The Wensum with a royal nonchalance
Shepherds his slender waters, yet the vision
Of vaster, upstairs doings takes his glance,
Patterns break out on humdrum ways to ocean.

You tell me all are as the leaping fish
And his silver devoted ripples, all are one.
Slave, power, your creative force and wish
Inform with praise the clouds, the earth, the sun.

*Francis Webb (1925-1973)*

## East Anglian Bathe

Oh when the early morning at the seaside
  Took us with hurrying steps from Horsey Mere
To see the whistling bent-grass on the leeside
  And then the tumbled breaker-line appear,
On high, the clouds with mighty adumbration
  Sailed over us to seaward fast and clear
And jellyfish in quivering isolation
  Lay silted in the dry sand of the breeze
And we, along the table-land of beach blown
  Went gooseflesh from our shoulders to our knees
And ran to catch the football, each to each thrown,
  In the soft and swirling music of the seas.

There splashed about our ankles as we waded
  Those intersecting wavelets morning-cold,
And sudden dark a patch of sky was shaded,
  And sudden light, another patch would hold
The warmth of whirling atoms in a sun-shot
  And underwater sandstorm green and gold.
So in we dived and louder than a gunshot
  Sea-water broke in fountains down the ear.
How cold the bathe, how chattering cold the drying,
  How welcoming the inland reeds appear,
The wood-smoke and the breakfast and the frying,
  And your warm freshwater ripples, Horsey Mere.

*John Betjeman (1906-1984)*

## The Waveney

Listen to me –
There is a little river, fed by rills
That winds among the hills,
And turns and suns itself unceasingly,
And wanders through the cornfields wooingly,
For it has nothing else to do, but play
Along its cheery way:
Not like great rivers that in locks are bound,
On whom hard man doth heavy burdens lay,
And fret their waters into foam and spray.
This river's life is one long holiday
All the year round.
Listen and long –
It hears the bells of many churches chime,
It has a pleasant time:
The trees that bow to it their branches strong,
Hide many birds that make its spring one song,
And orchard boughs let fall their flowery wealth,
To float away by stealth,
And land in tiny coves a mile below,
Or round and round the stems of rushes veer
Like snowy foam, but truly none is here,
So calmly gurgle on the waters clear
With endless flow.

*Jean Ingelow (1820-1897)*

## Tas in March

White on dark water, so stark
I leave my binoculars behind
and watch with bare red eyes

two swans, taut with sexuality,
stretching their necks
alternately side by side.

They are early: colour is
still to come to bone-dry rushes
and trees bank black strangling

their green. It is a hard wedding:
sharp brambles and ivy-covered
stumps hunch and hug;

sleet pokes the surface from
a blank neutrality, to come back
spitting with all its mouths.

Roused, the spread wings
beat their own storm towards
the north, wind against wind.

Somewhere in all this a small
heat is held, like the hope
of a cold man drowning.

*Edwin Brock (1927-1997)*

## River

You flow endlessly.
Over you your lights are beautiful – luminous and dark, moving and still, broken and whole.
In summer, columns of light – mottled by leaves.

In winter, the bleak light over farmland, the frosted-grey depth.
Today, in spring, lights dancing in and out of shadow – concealing and revealing.

In your course you are infinitely changing – neither crooked nor straight.
You fit your banks.
Running you are beautiful – slow in the deep pools – vociferous and fast in the shallows.

In private land you are hidden.
In public land you are open.
Beneath bridges you reflect back the faces of watchers.

In winter, you fill with water and become clouded.
You race between alders, pound through sluices, tumble over fords.
You wear a sullen expression.

In summer, you slow up and become limpid.
You display your weed in long floating trails.
You glitter past grazing cattle.

Then after long concealment your fish appear – sparkling-sided, melting and merging,
    vanishing and visible.

*Cameron Self (1962-*

## Stand in Late May

Take this manky ditch off the Yare,
this heat-stink of algae blooming –
what with all the ploughing to the margins,

abstraction of water, and run-off
into the marshes, there's such choked chances.
But in and about this scrutty reed,

here at least, a rhizal stand of yellow flag again.
Broadsword stems, forged from the sunk under
blades that splay to these blazing iris tongues,

each with the little zag of their nectar guide.
What's to be done but keep going?
The world is in such increments.

With so much more and more at stake,
I tell you now, for what it's worth,
here's where I hilt my every word.

*Matt Howard (1978-*

## Reedham Marshes

They say the water's salt here
as though the North Sea's fingers
are at our belly, tickling us like trout.

Dozy from blue and bottle-green,
we wallow in each passing wash
like a long drunk on a hot Saturday.

The reeds sigh and part as we enter them,
then zip us up behind like some
silk Sargasso. It is an old fantasy.

Sick from a seized engine, we sit
in this sanctuary of seabirds where
at night the crocodiles slip from holes

in their reed bed to jostle us
like hissing logs; and we confuse
the red rising moon with its setting sun.

Now no longer water-borne we drift
on this night mist which dreams us:
there are sharp cries, quiet splashes

and the voices of fishermen in an old pub
where a hand pours a White Shield Worthington
as clear as a bell and without a hint of mud.

*Edwin Brock (1927-1997)*

## Another Song of Another Norfolker

Bor, I never cood arn much money,
 No matter how 'ard I try'd;
But never wor short o' dumplins
 Or a good owd eel well fry'd.

Bor, I ha' found owd Norfolk frindly,
 An' I married a Norfolk gal,
An' when I cum off o' the marshes,
 I've found her a good owd pal.

Law! I ha' lived wi' monkeys,
 And worked where the lions roar,
But I longed tu heer t' owd curlews
 Whaup; front o' th' houseboat door.

So I drifted back tu owd Norfolk,
 And heer I intend tu 'bide;
For the bards, an' t' fishes, an' people
 Of Norfolk, air all my pride.

When Broadland is left for Jordan,
 And Charon cum over th' styx,
Du delve a deep hole in owd Norfolk
 Whose sile wi' my ashes shell mix.

*Arthur H. Patterson, aka John Knowlittle (1857-1935)*

## Shoe, 1979

I have this image of me
that's almost the picture
– gap grin, hedge hair, stripy-t
with long childish bones
on a log bench raised in a river
West Acre, the 1970s.
My legs are dangling in the flow,
arms angled, clinging on,

I'm surrounded by relatives
– and sometime before or after
the shutter snapped,
my white jelly shoe slipped
into the murk below.
I couldn't retrieve it.
Even if somehow it was there now,
it must have grown out of me.

*Heidi Williamson (1971-*

## Corpse Light Footage at Strumpshaw Fen

Look she says     look

& as if at her command
marsh gas igniting
under a lag of mist     bluegreen
aurora on a forefinger

her voice carries in the dusk
on the broken light she runs
her hands through

a train sounds     dolorous lur
or carnyx     between the horizon
& here a will-o-wisp
or local dybbuk pops

reeds sway in feather details
bats & may bugs fizz around
the silly thought that this all
is all for her alone

she climbs a galvanized cattle gate
her body a trig point etched
on the sky crissed with cloud

leans back & topples
into the grass smiling     breathing
hard     unhurt
what is it she sees there?

*Matt Haw (1988-*

## Breydon Way

Thank God for the eyes that see this lovely sight! –
The staring silence of the marsh, the green
Of deep water, the dark haven of the coming night,
The high pallor of the sky, the screen
Of trees like men along the Norfolk shore,
The little mills that catch the mind of heaven,
The tide that eats the sunset to the core,
A sunset shining like all hell forgiven,
This sheet of silk which skilful hands have spread
For water on a green unpeopled world,
Steep clouds of birds like vapour overhead,
The great circuit of horizon, pearled
And misted to the mood of dying day –
O thank God for my feet that walked this way!

*A.E. Tomlinson (1892-1968)*

## *from* The Broads, 1919

On Breydon Water, when the tide is out,
The channel bounds no sailorman can doubt
Starboard and port, the miry banks reveal
Where safety lies beneath its cautious keel.
But when the flood has wiped the water clean,
– Hiding the muddy haunts where seagulls preen
Their wings, and shake their heads – black pillars mark
The channel's edge for each adventuring bark.
Beware; the channel shifts, and now and then
A post deceives the hapless wherrymen.

*Hugh Money-Coutts (1876-1949)*

## Gone

Down in the dark water
Where the quick mill-race flows,
Something hidden rises,
Something secret goes.

Rising, it flashes whitely.
Going, it sinks below.
You cannot recognise it.
You see the water flow

Quickly under the mill-race,
Race down and reach the pond.
Whatever you have seen there
Goes on and out, beyond

Your vision or your knowledge,
Untethered to one place.
It glints, and hints, and teases,
And shows you your own face

Peering below the sluice-gate,
Watching the mill-race fall
Forever and forever,
With not a word at all

Of what you saw – or fancied
You saw rise up and sink
One moment in the water,
The next over the brink.

*Anthony Thwaite (1930-2021)*

# NORWICH & COUNTY TOWNS

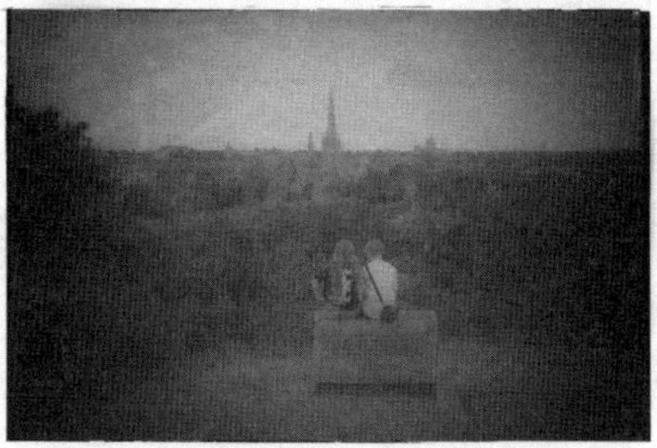

## On Tombland, or Empty Space

And since we pre-exist our names,
since land is land before it's claimed
for use, it isn't hard to stop amidst these streets
these houses & their timber frames & wonder
who lies here, beneath. Sleeping peacefully
or not. Or restlessly – taken by some older plague
more fatal than the ones we know now.
Whose spirits walk beside us, hungry
for glance or touch; a little laugh, a brief kiss,
a sympathy or a vengeance, unable to let go,
unwanting to step into the light until then.
What are the names of those who lie here?
Or rather, what are the ways that names lie –
tombland not as of graves or grave histories, but
something lighter than that, tombland simply
as empty space, or market place – free space to sell
& pitch a stall, years ago & still now. Time lasts,
or maybe doesn't. We come & go about our days;
we pass through them as flicking through a book:
each brick a word, street lane a chapter, reading –
without knowing – the remains of centuries,
finding nothing empty about this place.

*Victoria Adukwei Bulley (1991-*

## Bells of St Peter Mancroft

Gay golden volleys of banter
Bombard the clockwork grief;
A frisson of gold at the centre
Of prayer, bright core of life.

Who knew the old lofty tower,
The ancient holy eye,
To come open like a flower,
To roll and wink with joy?

Townspeople, who wear
Shrewd colours and know the move,
Now blunder and wander, I swear,
In a transport of love.

And the belfry, hale and blest:
Picture the jolly hand
Milking each swinging breast
Of its laughing golden sound.

*Francis Webb (1925-1973)*

## Norwich, Midnight

Sensing somehow earthquake or fire
creatures scurry through Mousehold Heath.
The moon snags on the cathedral's spire
as we walk home down Magdalen Street;

through the inner ring road underpass
the piss-yellow glow of the Oxfam shop,
in whose doorway we stop and kiss
kebabs in hand, with greasy chops.

Anglia Square has never looked so beautiful
littered as she is with burger boxes.
Praise the Lord and the City Council
down from the Heath come the urban foxes.

*Martin Figura (1956-*

## Thorns: Ironmonger, Tool Merchants, Garden & Home serving Norwich since 1835

From deep in the body of the earth comes iron,
by rail, by water, by horses, to the core of Norwich.
And two hundred years later my fixings and hinges
hold firm against tempest, flood, prying fingers
and the slavering maw of Old Shuck.

Come unto me for whatever ails your life
and I will furnish you with light
to reach wholly in your darkling corners;
to wait on you with findings for your tricolations.

I am the wunderkammer of practicality
bound to your service with every gauge of twine.
I praise the loyal wheelbarrow,
the steadfast ladder, oh faithful mophead!
Let us celebrate their ordinary splendour!

*Helen Ivory (1969-*

## On Anglia Square

It must have seemed a good idea to someone
To level Stump Cross to a concrete box
And let St. Botolph's sleep with all its slums gone
To ground beneath these steel-rodded blocks

It must have been a city planner's dream
To see these storeys shine with shoppers' cars
Sleek offices reflect the new day's gleam
An Odeon's steep palace to the stars

It must have seemed ideal, this blueprint vision
Of peacetime living – people in a precinct
Unstained by rain or rattled can or pigeon –
An Eden that would never need a rethink

Another Norwich, made of light and air
And not your shades and ages, Anglia Square

*Ron Nevett (1955-*

## Losers; Winners

*A small boy clambering up stadium steps for the very first time, gripping his father's hand, gawping at that hallowed stretch of turf beneath him and, without being able to do a thing about it, falling in love.*

So up those steps and out to scrambled senses:
Subbuteo men on baize, surrounded by heads
and hoardings, spurts of smoke, occasional hollers.
It's all so far away, all takes so long.
You've just turned seven. You know most of the rules

and never can wear that Liverpool shirt again
though Nan scrimped for it two long months ago.
No, now you're in the South Stand, Carrow Road,
Ray Houghton's been upended by Ian Crook,

and you are jeering, because the others are jeering,
and hugging your father's suddenly fatherly arm,
and waving the new inflatable canary
you'll later clothe, then pierce, and finally lose.

You lost. But now you're Norwich, so Dad is too:
you'll take the jokes and jibes for him at school
from glory-hunters in Arsenal and Liverpool shirts,
while he's at home five hundred miles from you.

*

And now he's purblind, and ransacked by thirty more years
of self-made battles: black-eyed women leaving,
and blackout drinking, then all those bottomless days
of pining for chances. That radiation scar
like chicken skin is not his fault. Nor the fear.

But what of the new young wife who's stopped being here,
yet suddenly owns his house, and all he had?
You scowl when people say he got what was coming.
And you're with his friend 'to tell your father the truth' –

not your idea, the friend's, who's cooked a lunch.
The three of you sit in cutlery-squeaking silence,
then two find the heart to try. And when it's no use
there's cheesecake, and Norwich on the radio.

That static as Teemu Pukki skips a defender
and finds the net is ten thousand hims and yous
applauding the way you couldn't those years ago.
You watch his eyes. He sees the same things you do.

Rory Waterman (1981-

## From a Window in the Close (Norwich)

Above the foam of pear-trees all in flower
The great cathedral rises like a rock
Out of the frothing sea, while on the spire
Perched as a sea-gull sits the weather-cock;

And in the pear-trees, in the silver foam,
The blackbird sits and whistles, now and then,
Such tunes as mermaids could not have surpassed,
Try as they might, to lure the sailor-men.

*Camilla Doyle (1888-1944)*

## On Norwich Castle

Our great cube was set cloud-high by the Norman
From Saxon trees, then continental stone
And soon its crenellations held each poor man
Without a coin or keep to call his own

But when the dungeons crumbled the Victorian
Swept out the cells and raised the chained portcullis
To light a glazed and galleried emporium
Of taxidermied kills and watercolours

Where as a child I feared the dried-out tiger
Who at a button roared in his dark case
But now I go to be a quiet admirer
Of Crome's soft clouds upon the water's face

Crossing the bridge of years to reach the mound
Of riches with which Norwich life is crowned

*Ron Nevett (1955-*

## Derelict Church

When earth and flint rear themselves into certain shapes
There is prayer from the fiery centre of the earth:
That grey dancer the belfry vaulting as the Host,
Arches as mouths importunate.
Dun smoking flames come leisurely home to roost,
The lost mind slews to an enigmatic path
Joining hands again, the errant spirit leaps
Into fire of joy at this grimy Fishergate.

Over the river's dank effluvia
Hang like launches the oozing sunsets, palls
Of light close dully. Enter this crippled church
To pray with a near-pride:
Cases are piled in the transept and the porch
Yet peace loiters here as not in cathedrals
While with advertisement and trivia
Man is besieging Heaven for his trade.

The Cross slopes down to jackboot and grimy truck;
Bones of the dead are indifferent to our debris
Grating above them; the devouring sin and pain
Still come to burial;
The immemorial Shape is persistent as rain.
Ghosts of bells chatter as from the sea
Out of memory slides home this gaping wreck
Still seaworthy, hallowed and functional.

*Francis Webb (1925-1973)*

## A Peregrine Falcon on Norwich Cathedral Suffers Delusions of Grandeur

O flat-capped priest who sends
homing-bound sacrifice
from his chicken-wired temple
to my Olympian perch.

They fly to me, cooing
their last farewell
to the urban-scape below.

I give them the time
it would take a condemned man
to smoke his last cigarette

then strike, de-feather on the wing –
a startled woman receives
a spiralling quill – brushes it off
like dandruff.

I take this offering higher
than he has ever flown before.
The blazing sun will never melt
'*my wings*';
then toss him to my love below –
oh, his life was well-lived –
plump, prick-skinned
little mortal thing.

*Sue Burge (1961-*

## On the Norwich Ring Road

Among the concrete
And litter of the central
Reservation, a
Tiny bramble has gained a
Foothold; sending its
Leaves out over the dented
Grey crash barrier
Into the fume-filled air, and
Here in this urban
Hedgerow it has put forth one
Shining, purple-red
Berry – which hangs its dark head
Inches from the speeding cars.

*Cameron Self (1962-*

## from Philip Sparrow

*PLA ce bo!*
Who is there, who?
*Di le xi!*
Dame Margery,
*Fa, re, my, my.*
Wherefore and why, why?
For the soul of Philip Sparrow
That was late slain at Carrow,
Among the Nunnės Black.
For that sweet soulės sake,
And for all sparrows' souls,
Set in our bead-rolls,
*Pater noster qui,*
With an *Ave Mari*,
And with the corner of a Creed,
The more shall be your meed.

When I remember again
How my Philip was slain,
Never half the pain
Was between you twain,
Pyramus and Thisbe,
As then befell to me.
I wept and I wailed,
The tearės down hailed,
But nothing it availed
To call Philip again
Whom Gib, our cat, hath slain.

Gib, I say, our cat,
Worried her on that
Which I lovėd best.
It cannot be exprest
My sorrowful heaviness,
But all without redress!
For within that stound,
Half slumbering, in a sound
I fell down to the ground.

Unneth I cast mine eyes
Toward the cloudy skies.
But when I did behold
My sparrow dead and cold,
No creature but that would
Have ruèd upon me
To behold and see
What heaviness did me pang:
Wherewith my hands I wrang,
That my sinews cracked,
As though I had been racked,
So pained and so strained
That no life wellnigh remained.

I sighed and I sobbed,
For that I was robbed
Of my sparrow's life.
O maiden, widow, and wife,
Of what estate ye be,
Of high or low degree,
Great sorrow then ye might see,
And learn to weep at me!
Such pains did me fret
That mine heart did beat,
My visage pale and dead,
Wan, and blue as lead:
The pangs of hateful death
Wellnigh had stopped my breath.

*

Like Andromach, Hector's wife,
Was weary of her life,
When she had lost her joy,
Noble Hector of Troy;
In like manner also
Increaseth my deadly woe,
For my sparrow is go.

It was so pretty a fool,
It would sit on a stool,
And learned after my school
For to keep his cut,
With 'Philip, keep your cut!'

It had a velvet cap,
And would sit upon my lap
And seek after small worms,
And sometime white bread-crumbs;
And many times and oft
Between my breastės soft
It would lie and rest;
It was proper and prest.

Sometime he would gasp
When he saw a wasp;
A fly or a gnat,
He would fly at that;
And prettily he would pant
When he saw an ant.
Lord, how he would pry
After the butterfly!
Lord, how he would hop
After the gressop!
And when I said, 'Phip, Phip!'
Then he would leap and skip,
And take me by the lip.
Alas, it will me slo
That Philip is gone me fro!

*Si in i qui ta tes*
Alas, I was evil at ease!
*Di pro fun dis cla ma vi,*
When I saw my sparrow die!

*John Skelton (1460?-1529)*

## This is the House the Word Built

This is the house the word built.

And the word was with God and was God
and the word was the house where the priest was,
where the friars, the abbey, the earth and the river,
the town and the sea and the sky was –
where the river reflected the town and the sky
and the house the word built.

This is the rich man who built his house where the word was,
his hall-house, his passage, his arch and his doorway,
his windows, his attic, his fireplace and screen-wall,
all in the house the word built.

This is the house the word built.

This is the smokehouse, the fish, the wherry and staithe
behind the house the word built,
the staithe that was built on sea and sky and river and music
in the town with the house the word built.

This is the trading hall, this the undercroft,
these are the dragons, the witches, the roofbeams,
the house of the treasurer, the property of the businessman,
the house of the mayor and mayor again
that was built with the money and fabric
the word built.

This is the house the word built.

And this is the property – the valuable rentland the trade-hall became
when the trader – the mayor – the businessman died
and sold it for the sake of his soul that he might
not be bound too long in purgatory
in the house the word built.

And this is the slow descent into poverty – into multiplication –
into tenements and foul yards – into cottage and labour –
into industry and intimacy – into river and sky –
into shoes into dresses into vests into brickstacks –
into one-hundred-and-sixty-five adults and children
in the grounds of the house the word built.

This is the house the word built.

And here's the first pub, The Three Merry Wherrymen – and here The Old Barge –
with its boozers and braggers, its buxom and ballocky, its bread and its bacon,
like all the great barges or ships of dead fools whom God the great word
sent on their way into broad bucking waves –
of the night with the scurvy, the syphilis, the TB, the ague,
all brewed in the house the word built.

Here's Agnes Palmer aged ten in mid-century, still here at eighty in 1911
and here's her dead father, and brothers: William, Samuel, Ellis, Edmund & John,
and here are the rags for rag-pickers, and here are the women waiting in doorways
in the house the word built.

This is the house the word built.

And here are the poor – stumbling dead-drunk down the alley –
here's crowds for the football, shopkeepers, bulldozers, slumclearers, developers,
the Old Barge still floating down the river of the word, into Dragon Hall
the city all changes, surviving in squares and streets
and houses the word built.

And this is the art that we live in and walk on and breathe in and pass through,
these are the doors of the word, and the words that pass through them,
this is our barge and our wherry and staithe and the words that we owe –
to those who first spoke them, since that is what art is,
the speaking of the house, the listening of the house –
to the voice of the house that's the voice of the river,
the sky, the sea, the music, the town –
of the house that we live in,
the house the word built.

This is the house the word built.

*George Szirtes (1948-*

## from *Autumn Sequel*, Canto XVI

And now to Norwich, to the Maiden's Head
Known to the Pastons but unknown to me,
As all of Norfolk is and so, instead

Of being what today it ought to be,
Norwich up-ends its yesterdays together
And overlaps its faults; where we should see

Commercial travellers talking shoe for leather,
Dead Benedictine monks and Flemish weavers
Intrude, intruding mediaeval weather

(Today was the first frost) while cumbrous cogs and levers
Turn twenty geese on one enormous spit
At a great fire, and fires yet greater teach deceivers

Not to be Jews or Lollards, till further fires are lit
By Cromwell's roistering troops to burn the books
Of Rome; till a German fat man signs a chit

For yet more fires in Norwich. As one looks
From the Maddermarket to Bishopgate, a broth
Of history garnished by ten thousand cooks

Simmers around one; calamanco cloth,
Cobbles, copper, pewter and blown glass,
Serpents and bass recorders and the froth

Of home-brewed ale, canaries, and church brass
Boil over while Sir Garnet Wolseley rides
High on a swinging sign and pilgrims pass

North-west to Walsingham and the night confides
Kett to the hangman's rope. Across the river
The tanneries deal with twentieth-century hides

While we, who have just arrived, ramble and shiver
Through an uninhabited Close where faintly whining
Ghosts beg their banished Virgin to deliver

Their souls from what dark verdicts hold them pining
Through centuries of purgatorial nights.
Mediaeval walls of knapped wet flint are shining

In mediaevally dim electric lights;
We wonder, trying to hold our memories fast,
If seeing sights means merely claiming rights

In some maybe maudlin, maybe mortgaged past.
Meanwhile, half way between the town and gown,
Between the older legends and the last

New learning, sitting at ease and looking down
Upon the cryptic relic in his hand,
There broods the statue of Sir Thomas Browne

Whose major object was to understand
The microcosm, who managed by the way
To make our language dance a saraband.

A Norwich doctor, basking in the ray
Of his invisible sun, prepared to eat
Frogs with the French and let his fellows pray

According to their whim, his mind replete
With curious questions and exotic riches,
Sweet rarities and charities, his feet

Ready to lug his wits through miles of ditches
Collecting and collating facts; and yet
This more than learned man believed in witches

And thought it godless not to. Without let
Or hindrance strange things walked his house, were seen
Scratching about his door, such things as might be met

In Norwich again tonight. For tonight is Hallow-e'en.

*Louis MacNeice (1907-1963)*

## St Mary the Less

In their time here
uprooted Huguenots, relieved
of home and a place to be,
urged hymns into apocalypse
for later eyes to witness –
a constitution of angels
quivered in the rafters, burning
to light all exiles home
in a frame of clunch and flint,
rectangular, aglow.

Today: YOU ARE HERE.
Items: one hole in the earth
where a blue denim rear
stoops over torn-up floorboards –
a rack of canvas seating –
a spread of plastic sheeting –
a patched-up pane, and muck on the cobwebs
where this art-work indicator
of some heritage provides us
with our precise position.

But Our Lady of Veils,
adroit at disguise yet
animate in each one, remains
at home, where you are,
for she's in you, sweetheart,
the refraction of desire.
Lady of Lack, pray for us!

Her goods preserved for sale,
this box of space she names
being at last a store

cleared for inaction,
her shrine may serve no longer
for a calling place, though none
the less she still persists
in absence, voicing need
as she always has and will
to the end. She keeps the quiet

on our account, whose inmost
heartfelt silence guarantees
some presence here.

*Glen Cavaliero (1927-2019)*

## The Return

(Cathedral Close, Norwich)

Long wandering years, you're past! – I'm home again.
  These winding alleys and these high flint walls
  On which the little creeping-toadflax sprawls
Have had the power to draw me back, to strain
Me close and safe – kinder than human arms.
  These bells whose leisured chimes ring in the hour,
  Not having changed like human tones, had power
To call from far through griefs and through alarms.

Oh, people change! I'm changed myself; but these,
These lanes for loitering in, these apple-trees,
  Gardens for reading in – yes, all I see,
The wheeling rooks, the tall stone gates that throw
Strong shadows on the quiet paths below,
  Are more myself than I myself can be.

*Camilla Doyle (1888-1944)*

## King's Lynn

Just opposite the elegant Custom House
So feasibly attributed to Wren
We watched the racketting pile-driver
Man-shouldered into place
By greasy caps and coats with pennant linings
Fluttering heraldic in the north-east wind.

Beside it on the quay a square-hewn stake
Extracted from the past – a broken tooth
Stained at the root – the crude support
Of civic splendour in the years of grace.

Explore now, as a freak tide might explore
This town that history could have made a city,
Swirl round the leaning pillars of this church
That could be a cathedral, then move on,
Inquisitive as water,
Over the docks, across the squares,
Into courtyards, under entrances.

Leave tides below, and climb
The winding centuries of a merchant's watchtower
To scan the wide way to the wider sea
For pennants fluttering in the north-east wind.

Step down to what the tides have left behind:
In the marsh-sunken chapel-of-ease
Two Dutch-scrubbed likenesses,
A merchant and his wife, as shrewd
And thrifty as the north-east wind,
Square-hewn,
Embedded in the local mud – essential
Supporters of armorial elegance.

*R.N. Currey (1907-2001)*

## September in Great Yarmouth

The woodwind whistles down the shore
Piping the stragglers home; the gulls
Snaffle and bolt their final mouthfuls.
Only the youngsters call for more.

Chimneys breathe and beaches empty,
Everyone queues for the inland cold –
Middle-aged parents growing old
And teenage kids becoming twenty.

Now the first few spots of rain
Spatter the sports page in the gutter.
Council workmen stab the litter.
You have sown and reaped; now sow again.

The band packs in, the banners drop,
The ice-cream stiffens in its cone.
The boatman lifts his megaphone:
'Come in, fifteen, your time is up.'

*Derek Mahon (1941-2020)*

## from *Poly-Olbion*

But now to nimble *Yar*, turn we our active Song,
Which in her winding course, from *Norwich* to the Mayne,
By many a stately seate lasciviously doth straine,
To *Yarmouth* till she come, her onely christened Towne,
Whose fishing through the Realme, doth her so much renowne,
Where those that with their nets still haunt the boundless lake,
Her such a sumptuous feast of salted Herrings make,
As they had robb'd the Sea of all his former store,
And past that very howre, it could produce no more.

*Michael Drayton (1563-1631)*

## Thetford

The poets, one and all, were wont to choose
Some fabled, fav'rite Goddess, as their muse.
But gratitude alone my mind inspires,
No other Muse my simple pen requires.
When erst in youth's gay prime and uncontrolled
O Thetford! round thy flow'ry fields I've strolled,
From Tutt-Hill's eminence and Croxton's height,
Have view'd thine ancient ruins with delight,
Thy sloping hills and wooded vallies gay,
Whose silv'ry Ouse meand'ring winds his way.
Though then, each lofty mound, each ruin'd tower,
Told but of war, and time's destructive power;
And thou, they pristine grandeur long had'st lost,
Nor more of Kings, or mighty chiefs could boast;
Yet heartfelt joys beneath thy roots I found,
And peace, with all the social blessings crown'd.
To tune his reed, and sing they healing streams,
Then enter'd not the Bard's enraptur'd dreams,
But now the Muse exultingly may sing,
The well attested virtues of the Spring;
Since erudition and clear truth unite
To chase all fear, and set the judgement right.

*George Bloomfield (1757-1831)*

## At Swaffham, 24th July 2020

We look for Keepers Cottage, find
the museum, its Carter room
'Covid secure'. *Tutankhamun's*
*Emporium* along the street
is run by the great man's great-niece
who asks us if we'd sanitize
before we go through the tea-room
to peep at the display: famous
faces, two thrones, wonderful bling.

For the selfie, our smiles are masked
as all expressions must be now
though only those of the living.

*John Greening (1954-*

## North Walsham

In a hotel in a small town in Norfolk I am listening to someone
throwing glass bottles into a metal bin: toss-shatter, toss-shatter.
There are no other sounds; it's a quiet afternoon
but the one tossing them has a sense of rhythm and I have
a sense that this has been going on for some very long time,
time being that medium through which we convey
the least knowledge of our circumstances to God, or one another,
which the body registers dimly in its cathedral of cells,
its telomeres, its intrinsically photosensitive retinal ganglia
that register the long days and longer nights of the blind.
There is pilgrimage and then there is direct action of the hand,
what Simone Weil called the 'iron' at whose touch
'there must be a feeling of separation from God such as Christ
experienced, otherwise it is another God,' toss-shatter,
the grasping and then relinquishing of the evidence of desire.
*I was perfectly happy there* said the famous writer of this place,
supposedly, when in fact it was a physician's surgery
(the physician was her friend; she came here to escape the city),
one young woman after another learning the art of venipuncture
and practicing it, for the public good. There was a time
when I had to keep track of which arm had most recently
offered blood. Outside a storm either is or is not billowing in
from the North Sea, from drowned Doggerland
into and over which I stared for several hours yesterday,
the Prussian blue-gray stain of the sky leaving the dark water
somehow lighter, as if possessed not of phosphorescence
but of resistance, a thunder-fetter. All afternoon I'd been followed
from ancient church to ancient church by two policemen
in a gaudy van; finally on some cliffs above the sea
I spoke to them, we exchanged cordial greetings and they sent me
on towards the bus stop at the outer edge of Mundesley
which, like Dunwich, is slowly slipping into that same depth.
I waited there with a woman and her child and a man who either
was her lover, or had been her lover, or—not the father
of her child—wanted to be her lover. 'Tool and a closed vessel'
wrote Simone Weil. I admire her notebooks so much more
because they force the reading mind to draw inferences,
to make the leaps she couldn't quite force herself to make
except in the fictions of her final essays, and in her particular
end, itself a kind of fiction, a falsified denouement,
all clues leading to both act and actor, in perfect symmetry.

For now we can pretend she was a character in a book,
her own book, perhaps—her own cave (elsewise Plato's).
She who abhorred choice, who wrote 'That is the whole problem.
To make time a moving image of eternity, for it is not so
naturally,' toss-shatter, toss-shatter. What was once the tallest
church tower in Norfolk collapsed here in stages,
1724, 1835, 1836, and was not rebuilt. I think about the fact
that Siegfried Sassoon and I both contemplated this
meaningless antiquarian datum, but also the exquisite tiny fane
at Edingthorpe, that reels in the light cast by the sea
and unfamines it, somehow, forces the intelligence back inside
its nude bottle. 'Make it so that time is a circle and not a line'
(Weil again) and 'Here are certain things which cause no
suffering whatever by themselves, but make us suffer as signs.'
She meant things like her Renault ID card, a soldier
in German uniform, a scrap of penmanship. A *hymn*
*veins the forest* is what I thought, at the time, and (*—I will have it*
*break my mouth*). What, then, of pilgrimage, that takes
the suffering sign and inscribes it over the length of the body
as a route, or, if you prefer, inscribes it *as* the body
over some distance in space, as a system of pain and arrival?
I admit I withdrew into my own small confession.
If like Weil we see God not *in* the injury, but *as* the injury
itself, the five Christs of Christ, each declaring its own gospel
according to its bloody lips, its bloody tongue—
A distant rectitude, where my book lay like some other
body I'd been wearing, or trying on, or trying to wear and then,
exhausted, set aside, too difficult, too meticulous for now.

*G. C. Waldrep (1968-*

## Flint

*Norwich meets its end.*

The sun disguises himself as a smoldering coal,
the moon has turned away her face, and gone.
How did it become so late?
How is it that the sky is now a sheet of iron?
How could it be rusted and dropping its crumbs?

My wormlings are gone,
my pebbles, all the little hoodlums. Where?

Look, the once-far Sea knocks on my door,
the once-far Sea leans like a mountain,
the Sea is a boiling line drawn up against my chilly skin. Since when?
The soil is syrup, the light is blood, the foul air full of foam.
It is late; I have been made to be alone.

No, *not alone.*
In the near-to I see *It*, and behind *It*, *It* drags the flood.

*You, You* stretch of gut,
slow crawling with dog's hunger,
*You*, and the red nail-hole of *Your* eye,
and *Your* oozing thunder, how dare *You?*
*You* godless grub, grot-skulk, grave-gannet!

Are we all gizzards for *Your* gullet?
Are *You* nothing but stalk, beleaguering, haranguing?
Black mold, answer us!
Don't *You* turn away,
don't leave us!
That sound, like brass and tearing,
that tremble-gaping in the ground;
my gravel shivers, the grass is afraid.
Bulks are rising, rot spouts, a bubbling froth of bone;
up come my plague pits, my potter's fields, my fifty churchyards –

the earth is giving up her dead

*my* dead.
Their star-bright skulls, I know them all by name,
and the numbers of those pearls, their teeth.
Where are you all off to, shining like that?
Why do you walk in a line? My loves, don't go –

but mud spat, glowing, they follow *It*,
little candles, creatures made of sticks,
and one by one are doused in the Sea, with a hiss:
in the hand-that-made-them Sea,
in the judgement Sea, in the end-of-the-endings Sea.

Must *You* leave nothing?
Not even their bones to comfort me?

How dark it is now, as dark as *You*.
In the dark I can feel it, the sheet of the tide
is sliding over me, pulled by a hot hand;

I hear Wensum's lullaby die away,
I hear the cathedral bell softly knocking
beneath a wave, once, twice, three;

the fen has filled with quiet sand.

Where have the stars gone? Where is the wind?
There is only water's cold tongue,
water's fingers in my pockets.

There is salt and sad caresses,
there is a silent mile above my head.
Where is this? I do not recall this death.

I do not recall.

Who's there?

*Cat Woodward (1990-*

# HISTORY AND PEOPLE

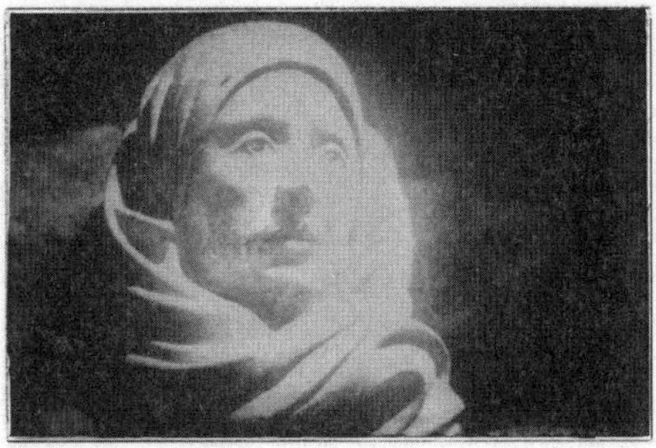

## Mother Julian, from Her Cell at Norwich

*By his grace I saw all this...*

Julian of Norwich, *Revelations of Divine Love*

I am not mad. Please do not believe me mad.
The lack of meat has whittled my senses to a sharp point.
See, I can write my name.
I know what day this is and which season.
I know how many bees make the honey
And why the robin's breast turned from brown to red.

The vision of Him was a smudge on the wall,
But the eyes of a fasting woman will do that sometimes.
He was handsome, I recall, even in the hour of His profound calamity,
When the flesh could no longer bear the pulse.

Do not call me mad because I think my hands too beautiful
Or a plate of leeks too rich a feast.
I draw succor from the flavor of contrition.
Modesty is the most savory herb,
Grace, the most delectable of sauces.

Sit, and I shall tell of a love enclosing.
First, look at the leaves of this mustard plant.
They are as splendid to my eyes as a pair of wings.

*Joel Allegretti (1955-*

## On the Airfield at Shipdham

*for R.H. Mottram*

There is the lark, you said. And for the first time
I saw, far up in the fast darkening air,
The small lonely singer beating its wings
Against the pull of the old and evil earth.

It is too late, I said, to praise its song...

Praise instead (because they bring our deaths
And thus another cycle of this bird's praises)
The beasts with guts of metal groaning on the line
Or in the higher sky solemnly muttering.

*Hyam Plutzik (1911-1962)*

## Near Coltishall

*for Michael Riviere*

Dark on the evening sky
(Though one gleams coldly bright
Caught by the sun's last light)
The thunderous aircraft fly
Into their deepening night:

Distracted from my page
I watch each passing plane –
The virtue of Montaigne
Is innocent to gauge
The wrath that they contain.

O privacy, retreat!
What fastness is secure
From that pervasive roar,
Who shall escape defeat
From what we dream of war?

(The village where I read
Is but a reference
On some chart marked 'Defence' –
Roofs overflown at speed
And of no consequence.)

Which would you choose, my lord –
The cant of government,
The smug cant of dissent?
Or would you turn toward
Your book's long argument
That wisdom is to know
How blindly we descend
To where no arms defend
Our ignorance from no
Imaginable end?

*Dick Davis (1945-*

## On *The Rings of Saturn*

This book is not about the rings of Saturn:
It starts in Norwich hospital and ends
Among exhausted Strangers treading patterns
From silken threads to try and make some sense

Of Suffolk churches sifted by the ocean
And silver herring heaped like no tomorrow
Grey photos set in prose without emotion
And Swinburne on the cliffs of ash and sorrow

Where living things take flight into the fabled
Like silkworms from their robes of soft black down
Inside the mind of W.G. Sebald
Who circles round the skull of Thomas Browne

His learned dust dispersed without a trace
Beyond the Norwich ring road, time and space

*Ron Nevett (1955-*

In digging up your bones, Tom Paine,
Will Cobbett has done well;
You visit him on earth again,
He'll visit you in hell.

*Lord Byron (1788-1824)*

## Kett's Rebellion

*The country gnoffs, Hob, Dick, and Hick*
*With clubs and clouted shoon*
*Shall fill the Vale of Dussindale*
*With slaughtered bodies soon.*
Traditional Ballad

One night last Spring
my headlights picked them out, –
long-shadowed lumps in a dip of the road
humped like refugees, everything on their backs,
squatting, or crawling like swimmers in mud:
it was the migration of toads
moving towards their spawning place.
'Can't be helped' I thought
and stepped on the gas...
spots of grease on the road flattened by daylight.

On Mousehold Heath they gathered
Kett's ragtail army, 30,000 peasants.
Below them the city of Norwich
trembled, a mirage in the summer heat.
Mayor Codd and his burgesses
flapping like chickens overcircled by a hawk
sent deputies bowing up the hillside
to bargain for time with bread and meat,
meanwhile sunk their valuables in wells
and out of a secret gate
sped messengers to London squawking for help
against Kett 'that Captain of Mischief'
and his 'parcel of vagabonds... brute beasts.'

For six weeks up on Mousehold Heath they sat
high on heather, sky and hope.
''Twas a merry world when we were yonder
eating of mutton' one would look back.
The sun poured down
and there was work for work-shaped hands, –
stakes to be sharpened, trenches to be dug,
a New Jerusalem of turf thrown up.
Hacking down the hated fences
and rounding up gentry was for sport.
Meanwhile the Dreamer under the Oak

wrote these words with the tip of his tongue:
'We desire that Bondmen may be free
as Christ made all free, His precious blood shedding.'
The sentries lay back on cupped palms.
Crickets in the dry grass wound their watch.
Clouds coasted round the edge...

'The country gnoffs, Hob, Dick, and Hick
With clubs and clouted shoon
Shall fill the Vale of Dussindale
With slaughtered bodies soon.'

August 27th, 1549.
A long black cloud against the blood-red sunrise
Warwick and his mounted Landsknechts showed up.
One puff of their cannon
took the skull of Mousehold Heath clean off.
Then down the hill they tumbled
with their pitchforks, their birdslings, their billhooks.
They had no chance, – less
than rabbits making a run for it
when the combine rips into the last patch
and the Guns stand by, about to make laconic remarks.
So they laid themselves down, ripe for sacrifice,
till the brook got tired of undertaking
and Dussindale was bloodily fulfilled.
Kett, found shivering in a barn,
was dragged through the city in ankle-chains
then hung upside down from the castle wall, –
they made fun of Death in those days.

Then Mayor Codd called for a Thanksgiving Mass
followed by feasting in the streets.
While many a poor cottage-woman
waiting for her menfolk to come back
heard tapping on the shutters that night
but it was handfuls of rain.

All afternoon I have been watching the swallows, –
black arrowheads flickering, side-slipping south,
using the grey air as a skating rink,
resting on poles adjusting their coat-tails
 or on telegraph wires, skittish music.
Some will crash in the ocean
or in the desert come to grief.
Thousands, finding the going too steep,
will perish on the shoulders of an Alpine pass
in scarlet-throated heaps, a black snowdrift.

*Keith Chandler (1945-*

## Boadicea, an Ode

When the British warrior queen,
   Bleeding from the Roman rods,
Sought with an indignant mien,
   Counsel of her country's gods,

Sage beneath a spreading oak
   Sat the Druid, hoary chief,
Ev'ry burning word he spoke,
   Full of rage and full of grief.

Princess! if our aged eyes
   Weep upon thy matchless wrongs,
'Tis because resentment ties
   All the terrors of our tongues.

Rome shall perish – write that word
   In the blood that she has spilt;
Perish hopeless and abhorr'd,
   Deep in ruin as in guilt.

Rome for empire far renown'd,
   Tramples on a thousand states,
Soon her pride shall kiss the ground –
   Hark! the Gaul is at her gates.

Other Romans shall arise,
   Heedless of a soldier's name,
Sounds, not arms, shall win the prize,
   Harmony the path to fame.

Then the progeny that springs
   Form the forests of our land,
Arm'd with thunder, clad with wings,
   Shall a wider world command.

Regions Caesar never knew,
   Thy posterity shall sway,
Where his eagles never flew,
   None invincible as they.

Such the bard's prophetic words,
   Pregnant with celestial fire,
Bending as he swept the chords
   Of his sweet but awful lyre.

She with all a monarch's pride,
   Felt them in her bosom glow,
Rush'd to battle, fought and died,
   Dying, hurl'd them at the foe.

Ruffians, pitiless as proud,
   Heav'n awards the vengeance due,
Empire is on us bestow'd
   Shame and ruin wait for you.

*William Cowper (1731-1800)*

## Bomber Base

The machines are quiet before the day's struggle.
Geometric lines subtend the air at random.
In the half-dark, propeller, wing and fin
Loom out of space. A searchlight lifts a far
Pillar of white and a flare falls slowly,
In isolation, so calm, so secretly.

There are many messages coursing the earth
In this wartime night: of command, terror, despair;
In guttural syllables, in soft, by lights in the sky.
And none so beautiful as the white flare sinking
On a distant field, in East Anglia the ancient.

And space is full of the mutter of engines passing
Over the clouds, like a great organ playing.

Now the thatched farmhouse sleeps in the dark
Among wakeful men, moving swift to their task.
The runways stretch silent; somewhere in the blackness
The guards stand, unseen, longing for home,
And a woman's arms, a warm bed in a house.
Upon the fields the stone weapons of dead men
Lie awaiting the outcome, which they will survive.
And the bomb-trucks move down the deserted perimeter
Where the cold North Sea wind stifles all.

Listen: the King's airmen are at large tonight.
But this is no story. Already the enemy
Touches them with his instruments. His guns poise.
Already fragments of metal puff out in the sky.
The bombs shatter the factory and many are blasted.
The broken machine crashes into the hill.
The young men die in manifold agonies.

*Hyam Plutzik (1911-1962)*

## Norwich Cathedral

The voice of Norwich Cathedral wells up from its root at the tomb of Thomas Gooding once every hour

You who *were*, like a curtain faintly parted, like the mute, vexing dark behind,
mere outline, once a creature of this digesting earth, a melancholy ligature becoming
solid, fluttering under the pin of a moment's brightness, the dote of prodigal Time,
rush onward now, mortify ground's jealous claw, spite the wind's inconstancy, you'll go
full clear of mortal tether, rarer than particles of air, and though you might dissemble,
find yourself in fearful Future's shallow hand, ended, you are not in truth,
so says I who tolls the time and tolls the time and tolls the time
so says I who tolls the time and tolls the time and tolls the time
find yourself in fearful Future's shallow hand, ended, you are not in truth
full clear of mortal tether, rarer than particles of air, and though you might dissemble,
rush onward now, mortify ground's jealous claw, spite the wind's inconstancy, you'll go
solid, fluttering under the pin of a moment's brightness, the dote of prodigal Time,
mere outline, once a creature of this digesting earth, a melancholy ligature becoming
you who *were*, like a curtain faintly parted, like the mute, vexing dark behind.

*Cat Woodward (1990-*

## Howard Carter at Swaffham

We know him: it's
the Carter lad who
painted dear Lady
Amherst's lap-dog

and the Vicar's old
bull-terrier, quite
without schooling – son
of our gamekeeper's son.

And if his imagination
pierces a tiny hole
in these venerable walls
and holds a candle

through to a room full
of wonderful things
but utterly foreign to
a decorously mounted

hunting party with
its fine equipage,
its whips and sticks and
stuccoed wooden courtesy –

then what is that to us?
Tally-ho! and on towards
the twentieth century: let
the boy be content

with keeping trespassers
from our noble pile;
or immortalise our
ailing Golden Retrievers.

*John Greening (1954-*

## On Margery Kempe

Untie your apron.
Delve into Christ's Passion, hear:
'What is your desire?'

Woman to woman.
Anchoress secures this soul
Steadfast in the sea.

Tears course down, enrage.
Bothersome woman keep on:
Tread your holy ground.

Come. Scold the Mitre!
Enflamed by Spirit – teach, preach,
You creature of grace.

*Revd. Ali Miller (1975-*

## To William Cowper

i.

You wanted to live
for always and always

if only to never know
what was beyond

Newton's determined arithmetic.
At Olney you watched

the leaves collapse
on the vegetable garden

and at Dereham you waited
over her blunt grave:

MARY UNWIN 1796
who could no longer

kiss you better, or praise
your stubborn hares'

hilarious leaps, your cauliflowers,
cucumbers, greenhouse.

Forgetful, her tender care
ceased. Her great child

cried his last poems
in the deepest gulphs.

His Homer rotted
on a high shelf.

ii.

I haven't been
to your grave yet,
that diamond of slate
our mutual friends talk of;
or Mary's square
in the north aisle.

I don't want that
self-consciousness
looking at graves of friends
brings to all my family
and I don't want
some good Christian

to think a light's
surprising me,
that a man's entering
a second time into his
mother's womb to
be born again.

Afterwards in
The Phoenix I
will drink the bitterest
beer, eat cheese and apples,
adjust these lines
again, again.

I am not sure
of anything
but the slow absorption
of germs, the loosening of
flesh, the sharing of
the bitter cup.

When Mary died
(they said) your cry
was 'not without emotion'.
A glass of wine. And later
your last words: What
does it signify?

*Fred Sedgwick (1945-*

## *from* Lines to Six-Foot Three

A lad, who twenty tongues can talk,
And sixty miles a day can walk;
Drink at a draught a pint of rum,
And then be neither sick of dumb;
Can tune a song, and make a verse,
And deeds of Northern kings rehearse:
Who never will forsake his friend,
While he his bony fist can bend;
And, though averse to brawl and strife,
Will fight a Dutchman with a knife.
O this is just the lad for me,
And such is honest six-foot three.

*George Borrow (1803-1881)*

## On Crome's *Norwich River: Afternoon*

Begin where curds of cloud and cooling blue
Fade willow into honey in the west
Beyond the Wensum and its Sunday crew
Who draw with dripping oars from all the rest

Of Norwich life, its smoke and gable ends
And brittle little fences made of sticks
To spend a sunny hour as airy friends
Afloat upon the mirrored chimney bricks

Then settle on the one who dips his gaze
And fingers in, but only sees the shine
Of shirt linen reflected on his face
As bright as brushed-in washing on the line

Still drying in the silver river, made
To hang as one grand plan of light and shade

*Ron Nevett (1955-*

## On an Etching by J. S. Cotman

*I wept to see the visionary man*
Dryden's Virgil

There is no richness in this scene,
No life to answer his abstracted stare –
And what we take it that these emblems mean
Is but the index of his inward care;

The summer-house will always stay
About to fall, the river make no sound
As Lethe-like it bears his strength away
And lapses to the darkness underground;

And poised above the silent flood
The couchant lion waits, a mask of stone,
Impassive by the tree that will not bud,
The spell-bound youth, beleaguered and alone.

The landscape is an open grave
At which the artist and his subject gaze;
When acid eats the plate, his skills engrave
Wanhope, a mind that falters and decays.

*Dick Davis (1945-*

## Woden

Masked and mounted
on an F-15
from Lakenheath,
he is cutting edge

circling again
and now again
Grime's Graves
where the spear began

its flight towards
flintlock, towards
no-man's-land
and moonscape.

How to clear
the forest and all
its fears? Dig
pits with seven

antler picks
to the flickering of
a chalk lamp
in the shadows

with a phallus
and a white goddess
heaving to give
birth to blackness.

Flint will carve
an opening along
the Icknield Way
and split the carcass

of Europe into skin
and guts and meat
and bones. What remains
will be what he owns

and is beneath him
as he spins thunder
from the cocoon
of his own silence.

*John Greening (1954-*

## George Harvey-Bone

That summer I spent sleepwalking
through mirror worlds of Norfolk seaside towns
in perpetual gloom, like a filter over a camera lens:
in Old Hunstanton
on the cliffs, I sat in the shelter
on the manicured green.

Next to me sat Mr George Harvey-Bone
who had *slipped out,* he said, *from evensong*
*where the choir sang like planes*
*going out across the Channel*
*and the stained glass showed ruins*
*of Coventry Cathedral.*

Funny, I thought
as Harvey-Bone went in '39
and has slipped from the pages
of that book.

*I'm looking for Mr Hamilton*
he said, *I want to know why I'm ill*
*I heard he's shooting up in Sheringham*
*but the dead aren't allowed on the bus...*
*... so I can't leave old Sunny Hunny*

He turned his head towards me
like a shutter coming down on a shop.
Staring out across
the phosphorescing Wash
I found myself saying
that if I bumped into Mr Hamilton
I'd be sure to let him know.

*Andrew McDonnell (1977-*

## The Dummy Aerodrome

Mist hovers in the fields and rises like incense
from a censer. It is a rain scant sky this September
of grey aeroplanes at night, coming in on a roll.

But over decoy fires and fake runway lighting
German pilots have crossed the North Sea,
past Yarmouth and Norwich, to find the real McCoy.

The dummy aerodrome, glowing like a hearth,
was built for this second wave of Messerschmitt,
the oil fire of flare cans and covert coal fooling

the raid of planes. A squaddie on the ground drips
creosote like candle wax onto the flames; fake smoke
of German bombs which tells the limber muscle

of Messerschmitt: Turn back, *you already hit us*.
Beyond battle simulation of target and strike,
things are made safe by the sprawl of fake craters,

the firing at lies. The past gets taken up by mist,
the stories that are told to machines built for speed,
to machines built for loss.

*Andrea Holland (1966-*

## That Thar Thorpe Rail Dissarster (1874)

Well, yew see that orl come about dew to confooshun
At Norrige Railway Stearshun

Wen the inspector bluk, he tell the Brundall trearn
To come down the track in pourin rearn

Just as the Londun trearn – at the same toime
Was a coming up the searme line

Ter Yarmuff. Well, they wus buth gorn farst
So wen they git to Thorpe – well blast

Thar wus a hooge gret crash
Wot sound like thunder and smash

Orl them thar carriages to bits –
So that int surprisin that it's

The wust trearn crash wot Norfolk hev had.
In fact, that wus so bad

That by the Yare side
That noight, twetty five people died.

*Henry Skipper (1943-*

## Dick Bagnall-Oakeley

This arternune I see the swallers flyin' by the pond;
They'a come agin, a-glidin' trew the air.
    An baads in thousands there mus' be
    A-comin' in acrorst the sea,
But he int watchin' on the maarshes there.

Them lovely golden plover, they're goin' on thar way;
They'a lorst a good ole friend, I reckon, bor;
    An far-orf where the gret geese fly
    The news is passin' roun' the sky
As he oon't taake thar pitchers enna more.

But life that keep a-goin' on; the bes' thing we can dew
Is call t'mind his friendly, wise old waads.
    Ah, yew an me, an savrel more
    Ha' got a lot t'thank him for –
A man what loved his Norfolk, an the baads...

*John Kett (1917-2010)*

## The Garden of Sleep

On the grass of the cliff, at the edge of the steep,
God planted a garden – a garden of sleep!
'Neath the blue of sky, in the green of the corn,
It is there that the regal red poppies are born!
Brief days of desire, and long dreams of delight,
They are mine when Poppy-Land cometh in sight.
In music of distance, with eyes that are wet,
It is there I remember, and there I forget!
O! heart of my heart! where the poppies are born,
I am waiting for thee, in the hush of the corn.
    Sleep!    Sleep!
        From the Cliff to the Deep!
            Sleep, my Poppy-Land,
                Sleep!

In my garden of sleep, where red poppies are spread,
I wait for the living, alone with the dead!
For a tower in ruins stands guard o'er the deep,
At whose feet are green graves of dear women asleep!
Did they love as I love, when they lived by the sea?
Did they wait as I wait, for the days that may be?
Was it hope or fulfilling that entered each breast,
Ere death gave release, and the poppies gave rest?
O! life of my life! on the cliffs by the sea,
By the graves in the grass, I am waiting for thee!
    Sleep!    Sleep!
        In the Dews of the Deep!
            Sleep, my Poppy-Land,
                Sleep!

*Clement Scott (1841-1904)*

## Mother Julian's Cat

I like to pad pad pad across the floor
Catch Her unawares
Invade Her contemplation
And send the hazelnuts skittering.

She would make a good cat.
She has the ability to sit and stare
To focus on one thing with absolute intensity.
She concentrates on a man attached to wood on the wall.
I sit with Her
Eyeballing a spider two inches to the left
And biding my time to carry out torture.

She is love and I am murder
But I'm mostly a gentle mass of tabby fur.
I rarely bite Her and let myself be stroked.
This is a necessity on the days when
She wants to break things or
Bounce off walls.

We spy through windows
Jostling at the gap.
She is rapt at the happenings round a table
And I gawp at mice.
Other times I escape over the wall
And do my own thing.
I return, reeking of the day's doings
She wrinkles Her nose, still buries Her face in my fur.
She scoops me up
My tail dangles and we dance a jig
As I purr out my adventures.
On serious days we have visitors.
It can drag and I liven up proceedings
With well-worn tricks.
I park myself between the two
And enjoy an elaborate frenzied wash complete with slurping sounds.
She rolls Her eyes.
Or I practise powers of petrification:
Those who are scared of cats sit very still
And become the perfect chair pour moi.
She smirks.

The last is potent:
Present the weepy sort with a freshly caught shrew
Innards trailing.
That gets rid
And then it is just me and Her.

We share everything
Even fleas and herrings.
Mostly I roll around and play as She unravels Her visions.
Both of us see in the dark.

*Revd. Ali Miller (1975-*

# RHYMES, EPITAPHS AND LIMERICKS

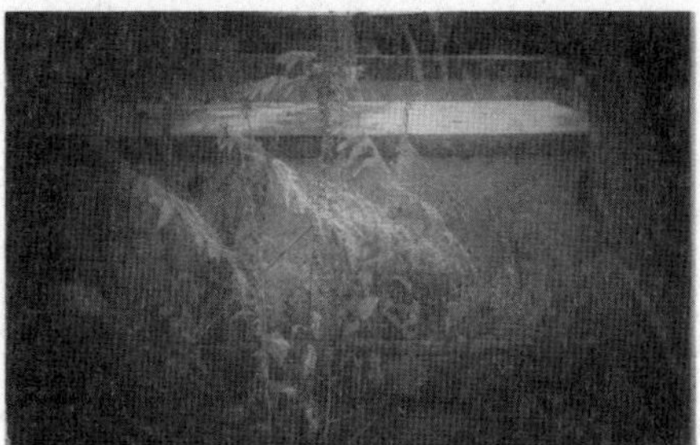

He who would old England win,
Must at Weybourne Hope begin.

*Anon*

Caistor was a city
When Norwich was none,
And Norwich was built
Of Caistor stone.

*Anon*

Rising was a sea-port
When Lynn was but a marsh,
Now Lynn it is a sea-port
And Rising fares the worse.

*Anon*

London, Bristol and Coventree,
And the Seven Burnhams by the sea.

*Anon*

All you that do this place pass bye
Remember death for you will dye.
As you are now even so was I
And as I am so shall you be.
Thomas Gooding here do staye
Wayting for God's judgement day.

*Epitaph for Thomas Gooding, Norwich Cathedral*

I with seven others went
Our fellow man to save,
A heavy wave upset our boat,
We met a watery grave.

*Epitaph for John Easter, Blakeney*

Not like Egyptian tyrants consecrate,
Unmixed with others shall my dust remain;
But mold'ring, blending, melting into earth
Mine shall give form and colour to the Rose,
And while its vivid blossoms cheer Mankind,
Its perfumed odours shall ascend to Heaven.

*Epitaph for Humphry Repton, Aylsham*

A monument to Rigby do you seek?
On every side the whisp'ring woodlands speak.

*Epitaph for Thomas Rigby, Framingham Earl churchyard*

Against his will
Here lies George Hill,
Who from a cliff
Fell down quite stiff.

*Epitaph for George Hill, St Peter and St Paul Church, Salle*

There was an Old Person of Cromer
Who stood on one leg to read Homer;
When he found he grew stiff,
He jumped over the cliff,
Which concluded that Person from Cromer.

*Edward Lear (1812-1888)*

There was a young lady of Lynn
Who was deep in original sin;
When they said, 'Do be good!'
She said, 'Would if I could!'
And straightway went at it again.

*Anon*

There was an old maid from Sea Palling
Who averred that today's youth are galling
'When I walk out at night
With my dog and flashlight
What we find in the dunes is appalling.'

*Keith Skipper (1944-*

Thar wus a young bor from Frettenum
Whose pants he were continually wettenum –
Yet despite his mum's shouts
He continued in spouts
And dint shew no signs o' regrettenum.

*Henry Skipper (1943-*

The man in the moon
Got up too soon
To ask the way to Norwich.
The man in the south
He burned his mouth
With eating cold plum porridge.

*Anon*

# CHURCHES AND HOUSES

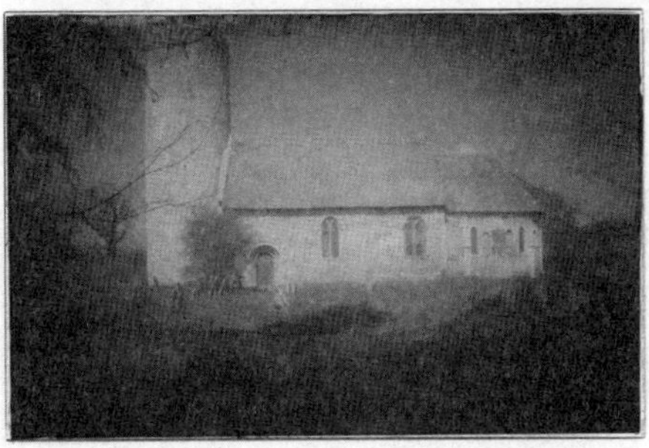

from *A Passion for Churches*

What would you be, you wide East Anglian sky,
Without church towers to recognise you by?
What centuries of faith, in flint and stone
Wait in this watery landscape, all alone?
To antiquaries, 'objects of research';
To the bored tourist 'just another church'.
The varied Norfolk towers could also be
A soothing sight to mariners at sea.

*John Betjeman (1906-1984)*

## Monolithicity

*for Blofield Church, Norfolk*

Knapped flint shines black.   Flint's kind.   Flint digged
from gravel pits                         where flint as neighboured
iron may show red seepage.                                    Flint
sourced from near the sea is grey. Like all flint knapped
it shines black.   Hand  over  hand  over  hand  over
a hundred feet        pre-electronic labour        placed
(not meaning to expose)    this basic grimness    faced
the rough sides with strips of knapped and shining
flintwork.                              The tower in a century
neared                                                   completion.
Now  is  the  tower  of  six  hundred  years  ago.
You could see it as one.   It rocks.   The bellringers
knees over head    scapulas over head    all hands
over ropes in a lifethreatening lightening   feel this
as charted colour   number   sequence   as pulled peal
and in the sway of stone in wind. The tower rocks.
Do you think it was meant to?   While the marguerites
make the white-capped ocean graveyard    meadow to
mast?

*Anthony Vahni Capildeo (1973-*

## Oxnead Walk

Ignoring the Private Property signs, we snoop.
Clamber on crumbling boundary walls. Find
lofty columns smashed and spider-strewn;
a kitchen garden still hosting sagging beds.

Earth-moving machinery buzzes. The rebuilt wing
rises, red bricks winking in the sun. Bare mud
will soon be turfed and clipped smooth, a venue
for wedding champagne in swan-white marquees.

In the church, under a marble coverlet lies
Clement Paston, builder of the house, neat-ruffed
and lush-armoured, ready to follow the blood-red
blaze of Henry VIII into France. High on the wall

I find My Lady Katren, dear wyef, with hair curled
and neck circled by pearls. She peopled the garden
with Venus, Cupid, Flora and Cerberus. Built a pagoda
with eight golden spheres. Died birthing her sixth child.

Us? All we have to do is to stroll back through
meadow grass. Avoid the nip of a curious foal.
Puzzle over the ragged flint tower. Stoop to
savour the scent of mimulus and mint.

*Caroline Gilfillan (1951-*

## The Church at Salle

*for Paris Leary*

i.

It rides the fields, superb, above decay;
ashen with age, its door will open
on to an emptiness so huge
it could let in the sky,
and so bright that prayers go blind
in the cold glare of its appalling day.

No angel trumpeters can ever sound
among these rafters; and the wrecks
of canopy and tester tell
of Word unused, unheard;
nor will old canny ghosts intrude,
for there is a great heathen wind around

and the hill slopes three ways towards the sea.
No humans here: the frail caul
of quiet is stretched across the stones,
pillar and buttress mirror
a mystery of mammoth whispering
invisible in grass and gale and tree.

What oracle? One sick and restive clock
gasps out unnumbered hours until
it steals the meaning out of silence...
But back in the swift air,
aghast at exile, still one feels
some answer waiting – had one the nerve to knock.

ii.

The flayed surface of the moon
sheds late light
across deserted pavements and the now-forgotten tomb.

The night sky sways
like folded velvet,
the Magi's star lost in the elaborate cloak of space.

Deep down, clay
mumbles in its sleep,
and slowly turns, blind to the blankness of the lunar day.

iii.

Lost:
in the dusk a hounded hope
scratches the dirt with chipped fingers
touching
a foresworn power
and the renewal of a kingdom's glory.

Found:
shorn of its name, the body,
uncrowned, is resurrected;
shamed,
is dragged to the cross of the young,
the buoyant church among the fields.

Hallowed:
in the dark of a good faith,
(shovelling the ground somewhere, nowhere),
beggared,
they watch a stoneless grave
engulf the remnants of their cast-off love.

Followed:
in a dead winter hour,
the claws of cold across their heart,
waverers
in a century's delirium
are stoned by the aloof stare of seraph eyes, apart.

iv.

Like a flail,
tearing across the gusty hedges
the gale crashes to a shock
against this hunk of tower
that swings the cold wet afternoon
like streamers, and whistles through its slats.
Ploughed fields are waterlogged,
and grounded aircraft squat like hulks;
cats crouch in the barn;
wheels scream at the lane's turn,
and the huge dead choir remains alone.

Stillness
of total space: only time
raps out its pulse
as the assault wears on,
as air and water whirl and toss in fury,
and earth holds fast on stone.
But underneath these towering timbers
above consigned, discarded bones,
the air contained is silence
holding the sphere's unbidden tune –
chords and bass-notes of the fugue of fire.

v.

The Reverend Whitwell Elwin built at Booton
(within eyeshot, a mile across the fields)
a church of Bath stone and local flint
to replace a shrine in danger of collapse.
He gave it a wide nave and narrow choir
(aptly symbolical of earth and heaven),
a sacristy by the font at the west end,
and a neat hut, commodious for hearses:
there was room for both the living and the dead.
The merry-coloured windows smile below
the august, if elephantine, angel beams,
and simulate the sun: a sound pile –
the gift of parson to his flock, the tithe
that affluence pays to want. A dream rioted
in pinnacles and crockets, spindle towers

and crenellated guttering – Victorian,
preposterous, and friendly as a face
in a top hat, awkward, angular, and kind.

The silver tower of Salle sails over tree-tops
as we drive about the lanes. Elwin could see it,
but ignored (wisely) such grandiloquence,
watching it focus mist or bear the stain
at sundown. He would ride or go on foot;
but now, set fast on plastic seats,
mere visitors arrive, all unprepared
by speed and preconception. Cameras snap
like stoats; but exclamations fret, and falter
at the enormity inside. Blank to our viewing,
this church owns itself, though dowered
by a queen's house; outgrowing piety,
has become the source of piety's occasion,
its whole shape and scale a perfect fact
and source of every fiction. Deeply dead,
it echoes every fear, and crestless soars
away beyond our hopeless eyes. The hills
it heralds have withdrawn, their bounding peaks
unseen through clouds of smoke-filled rain...

A scruffy butterfly flaps by the gate;
we hurry off, afraid of being late...

We shall not see Salle church again.

*Glen Cavaliero (1927-2019)*

## Written Amidst the Ruins of Broomholm Priory, in Norfolk

Broomholm, thy vaulted roofs and towers sublime,
Yield to the gradual touch of silent Time,
Whose luckless stole in dusky mantlings spread,
Veils the fair prospect of thy once famed head,
And all thy beauty now but dim appears
Through the dark backward of a thousand years.
Seared at the blast that hollow from the main,
Molests with sullen pause her ancient reign,
By the wan moon-beam oft the bird of night
Lengthens her feral note and wheels her flight
O'er the cold limbs that ever mouldering lie
Beneath the winter's wind and summer sky.
What though in vain with curious eye we trace
The tarnish'd semblance of the sacred place,
With eye profane its fading tints explore
That mark the features of the days of yore,
And fain would eager snatch from ruffian Time
The moss-grown fragment of a monkish rhyme;
What though no more at early dawn of day,
Eve's misty hour, or twilight's trembling ray,
With ken full blithe the mariner espies
Thy glittering domes and massy towers arise;
Far from the dizzy mast he looks in vain
And longs to fee his native shore again.
What though no scanty path we here descry
To cheer with foot of man the sorrowing eye,
Rough from the grasp of age thy walls deride
The slighter symmetry of modern pride,
Fancy, still fond, presents the long-drawn aisle,
And feels the brooding Genius of the pile;
Her magic spell th'emblazon'd arms supplies,
And gives the gorgeous pane a thousand dyes;
Rebuilds the trophied tomb of many a knight
With high hung helm and ponderous spear bedight:
Still the damp shrines a grateful awe inspire,
Pale burn the lamps, and rapt the stoled choir,
Still the loud organ's peal I seem to hear
That wakes the slumbering soul, and fills the ravished ear.

*Henry Headley (1765-1788)*

## At Thurgarton Church

*To the memory of my father*

At Thurgarton Church the sun
burns the winter clouds over
the gaunt Danish stone
and thatched reeds that cover
the barest chapel I know.

I could compare it with
the Norse longboats that bore
burning the body forth
in honour from the shore
of great fjords long ago.

The sky is red and cold
overhead, and three small
sturdy trees keep a hold
on the world and the stone wall
that encloses the dead below.

I enter and find I stand
in a great barn, bleak and bare.
Like ice the winter ghosts and
the white walls gleam and flare
and flame as the sun drops low.

And I see, then, that slowly
the December day has gone.
I stand in the silence, not wholly
believing I am alone.
Somehow I cannot go.

Then a small wind rose, and the trees
began to crackle and stir
and I watched the moon by degrees
ascend in the window till her
light cut a wing in the shadow.

I thought: the House of the Dead.
The dead moon inherits it.
And I seem in a sense to have died
as I rise from where I sit
and out into darkness go.

I know as I leave I shall pass
where Thurgarton's dead lie
at those old stones in the grass
under the cold moon's eye.
I see the old bones glow.

No, they do not sleep here
in the long holy night of
the serene soul, but keep here
a dark tenancy and the right of
rising up to go.

Here the owl and soul shriek with
the voice of the dead as they turn
on the polar spit and burn
without hope and seek with
out hope the holy home below.

Yet to them the mole and
mouse bring a wreath and a breath
of the flowering leaves of the soul, and
it is from the Tree of Death
the leaves of life grow.

The rain, the sometime summer
rain on a memory of roses
will fall lightly and come a-
mong them as it erases
summers so long ago.

And the voices of those
once so much loved will flitter
over the nettled rows
of graves, and the holly tree twitter
like friends they used to know.

And not far away the
icy and paralysed stream
has found it also, that day the
flesh became glass and a dream
with no where to go.

Haunting the December
fields their bitter lives
entreat us to remember
the lost spirit that grieves
over these fields like a scarecrow.

That grieves over all it ever
did and all, all not
done, that grieves over
its crosspurposed lot:
to know and not to know.

The masterless dog sits
outside the church door
with dereliction haunting its
heart that hankers for
the hand that it loved so.

Not in a small grave
outside the stone wall
will the love that it gave
ever be returned, not for all
time or tracks in the snow.

More mourned the death of the dog
than our bones ever shall
receive from the hand of god
this bone again, or all
that high hand could bestow.

As I stand by the porch
I believe that no one has heard
here in Thurgarton Church
a single veritable word
save the unspoken No.

The godfathered negative
that responds to our mistaken
incredulous and heartbroken
desire above all to live
as though things were not so.

Desire to live as though the
two-footed clay stood up
proud never to know the
tempests that rage in the cup
under a rainbow.

Desire above all to live
as though the soul was stone,
believing we cannot give
or love since we are alone
and always will be so.

That heartbroken desire
to live as though no light
ever set the seas on fire
and no sun burned at night
or Mercy walked to and fro.

The proud flesh cries: I am not
caught up in the great cloud
of my unknowing. But that
proud flesh has endowed
us with the cloud we know.

To this the unspoken No
of the dead god responds
and then the whirlwinds blow
over all the things and beyond
and the dead mop and mow.

And there in the livid dust
and bones of death we search
until we find as we must
outside Thurgarton Church
only wild grasses blow.

I hear the old bone in me cry
and the dying spirit call:
I have forfeited all
and once and for all must die
and this is all that I know.

For now in a wild way we
know that justice is served
and that we die in the clay we
dread, desired, and deserved,
awaiting no Judgement Day.

*George Barker (1913-1991)*

## Holkham

O come, and range with me th' inspiring glades
Where Leicester spreads the lawns and forms the shades;
On Holkham's plains bids Grecian structures rise,
And the tall columns shoot into the skies;
Beneath whose proud survey, extended wide,
New scenes, new beauties charm on ev'ry side.
Here crowned with woods the shaded hills ascend,
In open light there the low vales extend;
Here in rich harvests waves the ripen'd grain,
And there fresh verdure cloathes the pastur'd plain,
Sweetly intermix'd, and lovely to behold,
As the green emerald enchased in gold.

Lo, Leicester comes! before his mast'ring hand
Flies the rude genius of the savage land;
The russet lawns a sudden verdure wear;
Starts from the wond'ring fields the golden ear;
Up rise the waving woods, and haste to crown
The hill's bare brow, and shade the sultry down.
The shelter'd traveller sees, with glad surprise,
O'er trackless wilds th' extended rows arise;
And, as their hospitable branches spread,
Blesses the friendly hand that form'd the shade.
Joy blooms around, and cheers the peasant's toil,
As smiling plenty decks the cultivated soil;
The bright'ning scenes a kinder genius own,
And natures finishes what art begun.

*Revd. Robert Potter (1721-1804)*

## Felbrigg

*Remembering R. W. K - C.*

Families have no beginning, but can end,
Though three hundred and fifty armigerous years
Brighten the vellum. But life may descend
Obliquely, and a score of Norfolk squires
Are summed up here into a fresh dimension
That can progenerate outside the reach
Of county gossip and outlive the plantation
Of these long woods of Spanish chestnut and beech.
For a while over his arable and pasture
The rooks come idling home. The piled clouds glow
And fade this late October afternoon.
Here in his great library, ill and slow,
He leans between his lamp and the young moon,
Become the elements of more than nature.

*Michael Riviere (1919-1997)*

## The Painter of the Angels at Barton Turf

Long hours I worked, late into nights
when the milk of the moon lit my hand.

I had a team of painters with me –
bright-eyed youngsters and solid men

calm and capable with their brushes –
but it was my hand that drew the lines

that coaxed the nine orders of angels
into this church set in rippling fields.

One day, it seemed, the angels were empty
shapes, the next dawn they'd arrived

with a whisper of feathers, a hiss of silk,
on the good, strong feet I'd drawn for them.

They came clothed in scarlet feathers,
white ermine, rose damask,

smelling faintly of incense and lilies,
palm branches and ringing steel:

Seraphim, burning red with love;
Golden Cherubim, all-seeing;

green-winged Thrones, Dominions,
blue Virtues, devil-scourging Powers;

Principalities, Archangels in armour,
and Angels guarding naked souls.

All this was eight centuries ago
but still they glow in dappled light,

listening to prayers, readings and song,
and rooks and sparrows taking flight.

*Caroline Gilfillan (1951-*

## Narborough Church

I stroll across the railway bridge,
Past cottages with pink-wash walls;
My sentimental pilgrimage
Deposits me inside the church
As the chill autumn evening falls.

A seventeenth-century gentleman
Leans nonchalantly on his side;
His cold stone eyes appear to scan
The casual visitor who admires
The face that art has petrified.

A snapshot of the football team
Of nineteen-ten slants on a nail.
Some of these gawky youths who seem
Fit only for a rustic farce
Found graver parts at Passchendale.

This yellowing print, that crumbling stone,
Commemorating buried lives,
Might tell a saint that love alone,
When pride of art and body's strength
Grow dull and pitiable, survives.

But, standing here, I find it hard
To bandy such a word about.
Whatever flames grows cold and charred,
All self-consuming passion dies
And time stamps the last embers out.

My parents, married in this place,
I, baptized in this angel font,
Have left here not a single trace -
My father dead, my mother old
And I a mourning revenant.

The rags of flesh, the splintered bone,
Put off their lustre in the shade
Sooner than print or chiselled stone,
Though in the end time mars the bust
And the weak tints of sepia fade.

I walk in darkness to my car,
And drive along the narrow lane
That scores the landscape like a scar
To where my oblivious children lie
Cocooned by sleep from wind and rain.

*John Press*
*(1920-2007)*

## The Deserted Church Tower on Sidestrand Cliff

Oh! once I had a clamorous bell
The villagers all knew so well
That through my porch they drifted in;
To learn the ways of shunning Sin.
For 'Love wide as the Sea' their quest,
For 'Peace' and 'Everlasting Rest!'
They sang and sat with one accord,
The preacher preached, the elders snored,
The children fidgeted and played
And each young man eyed each young maid,
Till when he came to 'Glory be...'
All rose, and drifted out of me!

My bell is gone, my porch is down;
Through my void windows now is blown
By every wind the day may send
The breath no preacher now will spend.
The young and old are here in rows,
Where, flowery tall, the sweet hay grows;
They neither fidget now nor snore,
The young men eye young maids no more;
They come not, go not, soon or late,
But with me, on the cliff-edge, wait.
Seaward we slip, and seem more fain
To be 'washed clean' and 'born again'!

*R.H. Mottram (1883-1971)*

## At Swanton Morley in the Spring

It seemed to us the church had just alighted,
lowered to earth by flexed seraph muscles.
Blithe on a springboard day it strained, it leaped
up like the lambs or the village children swinging:
arches stretched, timbers braced, it'll soon be off and flying.

April scurries around these watery pastures
bringing the smell of violets to the sea;
it hums like a bee in the clap-boards of the belfry.
We clamber about the mound of heather, flowerless
marking the airman's grave, tougher than young Narcissus.

War's lover, twenty-eight years he lived
and twenty-eight he's mouldered: marsh miseries
render the mourners soggy, apprehensive.
Oh dire spring greeting! The primrose pains
and the lent lily stabs at us in yearly barbed offensive.

Be warned: clouds in a hurry are tugging at the tower;
lichen, gusty, longs to be launched – now!
The angels are coming! Stones stamp, winged. Up,
the bulked choir neighs, sings to us, climb, be killed!
(Trampling the limp memorials, all the holy sulking.)

*Glen Cavaliero (1927-2019)*

## Winter Farmhouse

builds itself out of deepest dark.
Under a pelt of thatch and frost
chamfered bone shivers in the wind,
shivers in the eastern wind.

We shrink into otherness; our fingers whiten.
The house is our nest of apprehension,
a cavern of ash and sighs where rats tap-dance

as Daisy, Dapple, patched out of moonlight,
strike flown sparks from tumbled cobbles,
whinny in the break and tangle of our dream.

We had not known the inside was so out,
the droves of night so full of watching,
the out so in, swung doors at sentry-go

as the dead with owl-faces and bleak eyes
busy with milk-pails, whips and ribbons
cross sill and threshold in a dry-leaf hush.

The cold, such cold
where cats creep out of their garden-graves
to keen in the wind,
to keen in the eastern wind.

*Peter Scupham (1933-2022)*

## On a Rood-Screen in Worstead, Norfolk

I sing a saint of Portugal,
  Her name is Saint Uncumber,
And heaven does not hold a more
  Resourceful little number.

She kept a snow virginity
  And when a satyr neared,
To foil his suit, became hirsute
  And grew herself a beard.

Homage to thee, Uncumber
  Thy legend is seductive,
And pilgrims turning Worstead way
  Will find it most instructive.

*Kit Wright (1944-*

## Tottington: Reredos

of stone, in St Andrew's church; a Baronet's row of thanks
in the lifting of the weight of typhoid from a young son,
the ornamental retable a gift left behind in a vacant church
for God to look over the empty aisle.

The bells will go to Seasalter. The rood screen remains,
a stained glass plump with angels, hums *ecce, sanctus, filius.*
The pulpit, hassocks and dog-headed pews full of worm
are also lifted out and left leaning in pieces.

The piscina is in hiding and the corbels are minus their heads.
Lucilla polishes the plaque for Frederick Worby, *killed in France*
in 1917. She watches the church be taken down, *stacked against*
*the damp walls, in the way of the cleaners.* The firm horsehair broom

before the woman's feet swishes away nibs of mud
from army boots and brushes at dead flies; as the sturdy
horse once lifted its tail and shook his head at the scimitar
mandible, the persistent bite of the Brown Edged Emperor,

the Cleg and Soldier flies.

*Andrea Holland (1966-*

## On Lady Katharine Paston's Tomb at Oxnead

Sun set three hundred years,
These marble shadows on the wall still stand,
Fixed by her husband's grief, and Stone's hand,
Long-vanished skill, and wealth, and tears.

Outside her dilapidated
Church the usual June again transposes
The graveyard offals into grass and roses,
Beauty and corruption equated,

Balanced principles,
Whereby this white *memento-mori* is
Now mere *memoria pulchritudinis*,
New summer dappling her walls.

We're not the tomorrow, alas,
Of this lady's wish; her treasures scattered for ever,
Her mansion now green mounds beside the river,
Not a Paston left to wear her flesh ...

And since we put the resurrection
Even of annual crops to chance,
Eternity of blood's no longer, as once,
Any man's confident possession.

We do with less than that:
The uncertain hope that someone not yet born
May saunter here on a remote June morning
To find the key under the mat.

*Michael Riviere (1919-1997)*

# LANDSCAPE

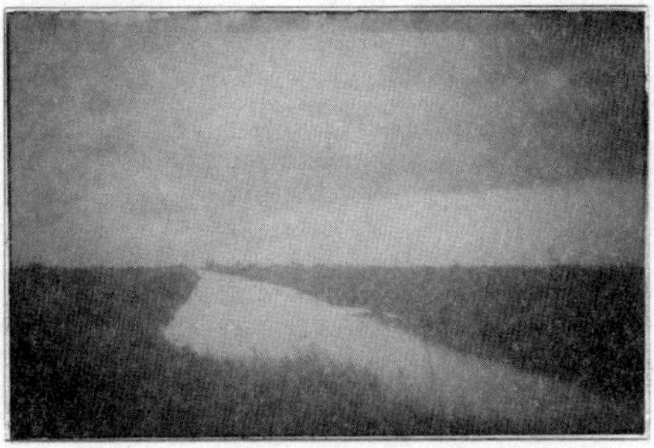

## Rural Scene

The luminous Norfolk skies,
the tractors, the gunshots,
the still ponds, the darting rabbits,
cow parsley by the field gates –

all are re-imagining themselves
because Tariq walks in his village,
part of the scene, yet conspicuous
as if he is walking a tiger.

*Moniza Alvi (1954-*

## Our Lady of Walsingham

There once the penitents took off their shoes
And then walked barefoot the remaining mile;
And the small trees, a stream and hedgerows file
Slowly along the munching English lane,
Like cows to the old shrine, until you lose
Track of your dragging pain.
The stream flows down under the druid tree,
Shiloah's whirlpools gurgle and make glad
The castle of God. Sailor, you were glad
And whistled Sion by that stream. But see:

Our Lady, too small for her canopy,
Sits near the altar. There's no comeliness
At all or charm in that expressionless
Face with its heavy eyelids. As before,
This face, for centuries a memory,
*Non est species, neque decor.*
Expressionless, expresses God: it goes
Past castled Sion. She knows what God knows,
Not Calvary's Cross nor crib at Bethlehem
Now, and the world shall come to Walsingham.

*Robert Lowell (1917-1977)*

## Morning in Norfolk

As it has for so long
come wind and all weather
the house glimmers among
the mists of a little
river that splinters, it
seems, a landscape of
winter dreams. In the far
fields stand a few
bare trees decorating
those mists like the fanned
patterns of Georgian
skylights. The home land
of any heart persists
there, suffused with
memories and mists not
quite concealing the
identities and lost
lives of those loved once
but loved most. They haunt it
still. To the watermeadows
that lie by the heart they
return as do flocks of swallows
to the fields they have known
and flickered and flown so
often and so unforgettably over.
What fish
play in the bright wishing
wells of your painted
stretches, O secret
untainted little Bure,
I could easily tell,
for would they not be
those flashing dashers
the sometimes glittering
presentiments, images
and idealizations
of what had to be?
The dawn has brightened the
shallows and shadows and
the Bure sidles and idles
through weed isles and fallen

willows, and under
Itteringham Mill, and
there is a kind of rain-
drenched tittering in the
air, the night swan still
sleeps in her wings and over it all
the dawn heaps up the hanging
fire of the day.

Fowell's tractor blusters
out of its shed and drags
a day's work, like a piled sled
behind it. The crimson
December morning brims over
Norfolk, turning
to burning Turner
this aqueous water colour
idyll that earlier gleamed
so green that it seemed
drowned. What further
sanction, what blessing
can the man of heart intercede for
than the supreme remission
of dawn? For then the mind
looking backward upon its
too sullied yesterday,
that rotting stack of
resolution and refuse,
reads in the rainbowed sky
a greater covenant,
the tremendous pronouncement:
the day forgives.

Holy the heart in
its proper occupation
praising and appraising this
godsend, the dawn.
Will you lift up your eyes
my blind spirit and see
such evidence of
forgiveness in the heavens
morning after golden
morning that even
the blind can see?

*George Barker (1913-1991)*

## Thetford Forest

Frozen mud-pelt of early morning,
the air bristles with frost-shine.

Our winter breath hangs
in the air before us.

We walk into deep grey
where the trees crowd in,

their pine needle smell
overwhelming.

There is faraway bird-call,
the startled flap of a fresh waked pigeon,

A deer eye appears,
and vanishes back into shadow.

We emerge into the stark-limbed skeleton
of the deciduous forest.

The sky opens out – a gap of relief
after the inky conifers.

We gulp lung after lung of early winter,
see every third tree marked with a cross:

a yellow smear
where the saw will bite,

flaking jackets of bark barely
covering pale bodies.

*Julia Webb (1966-*

## The Brecks

A broken land
Of sand and flint
And heath and heather

Where once the rabbit was king
And fields reverted back
Or blew away

Neither here nor there
Our very own Dust Bowl
Baking and freezing

Where warrens bequeathed
Placenames and where Thetford Forest
And pig houses

Now hold it all in place
A peculiarity seen from a car window
On the A11 – but

Suddenly revalued today
This ancient landscape
Coming into focus

Like a deer glimpsed
Through the prism
Of twisted pines

*Cameron Self (1962-*

## Brecks

The soil is half sand, silent
and the colour of sparrows.
Spring fills in the gaps, marks
hedges and tilth. Wind sounds
through fields without regret
for the time it took to get here.
Someone is ploughing, someone
is crying. The plan is to slowly
break up the soil. The plan is to live
as best as one can using cultivators,
harrow and the sweep of the scythe.

*Andrea Holland (1966-*

## Lammas

When I say *they are cutting the barley*
I am speaking a dead language.
What does it signify? They: are cutting:
the barley: at most an image
out of a car window,
a machine in the corn,
as remote as (also dead) *Lammastide*.

At new year, at this new year,
a conjecture, *it is thought*
the ancestors got drunk on old beer,
ate new baked barley cake, put a boy
in a basket, cut his throat, burned him to ash –
first fruits.
Also remote (all, so).

When I say *they are cutting the barley*
I have in mind various stories,
images, a girl of ten years
holding the neck of a horse,
kissing the face of the horse; or
stooks, stacks,
threshing, (further away are 'flails').

The barn has doors north and south: that way
the wind clears the chaff. The house
has a foot of chaff packed between floor
and ceiling, ceiling and roof space,
a ladder to the attic –
*the hired girl slept with the apples* –
this is also conjecture, a fiction.
Whoever she is she steps out, midday
with the dark ewers of alcohol
(where are we now?) to find the men.
They are not mowers with scythes;
all they have is hooks,
sickles (sharp
the cut stubble spikes at her ankles).

You will not see her from the motorway,
she might be you, Ruth, not
sure, really, yet. While the men drink
she picks at the skin on her wrist,
stares at a stone on the ground;
all this done much as a
snake licks at the air.

And is this so terrible? A language
invents (love, death, a journey: but my dear
the dead boy is real). Is the field
clear for the moon to rise?
The barley is cut and carted,
the women have milled
a coomb sack of it.

*Michael Mackmin (1941-*

Sweet was the walk along the narrow lane
At noon, the bank and hedge-rows all the way
Shagged with wild pale green tufts of fragrant hay,
Caught by the hawthorns from the loaded wain,
Which Age with many a slow stoop strove to gain;
And childhood, seeming still most busy, took
His little rake; with cunning side-long look,
Sauntering to pluck the strawberries wild, unseen.
*Now*, too, on melancholy's idle dreams
Musing, the lone spot with my soul agrees,
Quiet and dark; for through the thick wove trees
Scarce peeps the curious star till solemn gleams
The clouded moon, and calls me forth to stray
Thro' tall, green, silent woods and ruins gray.

*William Wordsworth*
*(1770-1850)*

## On Caistor St Edmund

*Caistor was a city when Norwich was none,*
*Norwich was built of Caistor stone*

Anon

On wildflower walls a fading legionary
Surveys the Norwich–London train's straight line
Unseen by sheep who chew the greenery
Inside their quadrant's crumbling flint and lime

One year the barley glowed with road and alley
And showed the airman Venta Icenorum
Was not an idle story of the valley
But clay and timber: temple, baths and forum

And citizens, like Nase who scratched a lead scroll
To offer Neptune leggings for a thief
Or those who played with bones or broke a red bowl
And wore the sunlight on them like gold leaf

And heard an empire passing with a shiver
And turned to grass and earth beside Tas river

*Ron Nevett (1955-*

## Welney

Suddenly East Anglia is green again. The silver green of barley fields, the tufty green of meadows broken by the yellow remains of last year's rushes, the square woods of field boundaries, the new leaves lighter green, the crude plastic blue of a distant portaloo for field workers, a celestial apartment, a fenland tardis.

A year shuffling back and forth between cities on a near empty train, through small towns starting to wake up, isolated fen houses; embargoed ships tethered to the landscape, and everyday there is something new, and the country like the city is always changing, nothing is ever finished, things seemingly disappear.

So it goes, moment to moment, seemingly random. What do you do with the space they leave, the gap where a building once stood, the place where there used to be a huge apple tree? Light fills it, the moment is new, yet loss interferes with each moment; gives it a shape like one of those magic eye pictures of dolphins appearing from garish fractals.

You stare too long and you see more than you want to. So you have to shake it off, a dog shaking the scent of a stranger's hand. There are things to be done, emails to answer, tickets to show, books to be read, essays to mark. The landscape is just green, it is morning, spaces are filled with light.

*Andrew McDonnell (1977-*

## The Fen

No more I hear the waters roar,
Roused by the coming of the bore,
No more the river turns again
To sweep across the level fen –
No more the winds in fury ride
Above the marshes wild and wide
Before the rising of the tide:
The waters roam no more.

No more I wade along the fen
For heron or for water hen,
Nor hug the bottom of my boat
As to the feeding ducks I'd float;
Nor ambushed lay wi' roving eye
To watch like specks against the sky
The wild geese circling on high:
The waters roam no more.

No more I creep, nor crouching, run,
Nor trail my owd long-barrelled gun,
Nor listen how the water laps
About my sunken fishing traps;
'Tis eighty year sin', as a boy,
I first helped at the duck decoy,
And now – I know but little joy:
The waters roam no more.

My feyther knew the hidden ways
Across the waste and marshy maze;
He knew each haunt of bird and fish
And how to find 'en at his wish,
While sometimes in his punt he'd sing
Until the reedy dykes'd ring,
But now's the end of everything:
The waters roam no more.

When, on a stormy winter's night
There stirs a noise, or sudden light,
I lay and pant to hear 'em shout
In panic 'coz the water's out;
For long I look and anxious strain;
Alas! my hope is allers vain,
And sad I go to sleep again:
The waters roam no more.

No more the waters roam on land,
But hid away on every hand
Are led in channels to the sea;
Instead of flowing fancy free,
Instead of roaring fierce and wild,
The same as when I wor a child,
They creep imprisoned and defiled:
The waters roam no more.

*Bernard Gilbert (?)*

## Yuletide in Norfolk

The long-ships drove up the Bure, and the horned men were
 there to rape and to burn,
Seeding their names, Rollesby and Billockby, Fleggburgh,
 Clippesby and Thurne,
Ashby and Oby. Our church roofs came from the rot of each
 oak-warped stern.

But the Nazarene grip was strong. The surge of energy in
 the whoring blood
Settled for the purpled moan of the organ, the heifer
 chewing her cud,
And the cart with its thwarted axle broken and stuck in
 December mud.

I drive to the service at Clippesby, a mile along
 sugar-beet-sodden-road.
My lights throw up the parishioners, whipped by the
 Christian goad
And the hope of Heaven, their faces pinched by a cold,
 unearthly woad

Into shapes of bread and wine. Their archangels gloat and
 wither on spruce,
Bald winter's fuel from Norway. The tied surplice is
 shaken loose,
And the paean rises, the bitter semen of prayer squeezed
 like a juice.

Nothing can alter the sounded heritage from the
 throbbing brine,
The keels lifting above the waves. Let humility
 be divine.
All arrogance is human, the black ride of the Vikings
 is mine.

*George MacBeth (1932-1992)*

## Norfolk

Sand-martins whirling out of cliffs.
Hay trussed in roly-poly bales.

Stalled windmills. Big skies.
A place for weather-watching rites, for money

to invest in, rewarding itself
with the obligatory boat and a lawn

that tapers off in search of water, life's
elixir, leisure's mirror... Walsingham

and Cromer: the manufactured shrine with
something – nothingness? – candled at its heart,

the deft resort with one eye on your wallet
and one on the enigma of the sky

that bends above the threatened beach
where if, as they heap and spill, drag and heap,

the waves are trying to communicate –
some maxim, perhaps concerning survival,

the need to endure, to hope just enough –
you find you're baffled, you can't hear a word.

*Michael O'Neill (1953-2018)*

## Invocation

Who fashioned this land of fields, fen-man
Clawed from beneath the sea's tongue?

Who drained these lost levels, fen-man
With lock and sail and engine?

Who sweated knee-deep in the fen mud,
Exhausted by the clod weight

And the singing of the wind's voice?
Why, you did!

But who filled your brain with peat?
Who cast the speech from your blue tongue?

And who, after stealing your five senses
Left you, wedged and breathless

Under your own sky?
Why, the land did, the land did!

*Cameron Self (1962-*

## from *Piers Plowman*

Pilgrimes and palmers plihten hem togederes
For to seche Seint Jame and seintes at Roome;
Wenten forth in heore wey with mony wyse tales,
And hedden leve to lyen al heore lyf aftir.
Ermytes on an hep with hokide staves,
Wenten to Walsyngham and here wenchis after;
Grete lobres and longe that loth weore to swynke
Clotheden hem in copes to beo knowen for bretheren;
And summe schopen hem to hermytes heore ese to have.

*William Langland (1336-1386)*

## Dimensional stability

The way, for example, paper
retains its self despite
damp or heat or frost,
or a bird continues to flit
on altered airstreams.

*

Out here in the damp margins
flint fractures the fens' panorama
with bright towers of churches
primed to call out if the sea
visits, without warning,

the sites of special scientific interest:
the heath of silver-studded blues;
woodland where the pool frogs spawn;
lagoons where starlet sea anemones
practise their minute fission.

Instead, the sea deftly extends
its lips to the land, worrying
stone into flecks of sand:
all substance carried under,
like the story of the lost town

submerged into history,
the lungs of its chapel replete
with creatures. The stone floor
of its aeons-old sea burgeoning
beneath the new town, unsettled.

Even now I hear the creak-crack
of the pill boxes, rusting their way
towards France, their iron bars released,
as the houses and people and matter
progress and regress.

*

The way, for example, the ocean,
freeing itself of its borders,
falls constantly into its element:
its heedless waters closing
over our mouths.

*Heidi Williamson (1971-*

## Backwaters: Norfolk Fields

*for W.G. Sebald*

1.

Backwaters. Long grass, slow speech. Far off
a truck heaves its load of rust into a yard
next to a warehouse full of office furniture
no one will ever use, unless to stuff
some temporary room when times are hard.
Across the fields the sweet smell of manure.

We're years behind. Even our vowels sag
in the cold wind. We have our beauty spots
that people visit and leave alone, down main
arterials and side roads. A paper bag
floats along the beach, clouds drift in clots
of grey and eventually down comes the rain.

We're at the end. It might simply be of weather
or empire or of something else altogether.

2.

Empire perhaps. Chapels in the cathedral.
Old airstrips. History's human noises
still revving down a field. Clothes pegs hang
like hanged men. It is all procedural.
Resentment simmers in the empty houses.
The wind at its eternal droning harangue.

I'm wanting to mouth the word that fits the case
but it's like trying to roll a shadow from
the street where it has been sitting for years.
It will not go. You cannot wipe the face
of the clock or restore a vanished kingdom.
You feel the shape of the thing between your ears.

Your mouth is talking to the steady light
which listens to you and remains polite.

3.

How beautiful the place is. Watch it hold
time still. I want you to tell me what this is,
this place at the back of beyond, in the sun
that retains its distance in a pale gold
mirror, minding its own brilliant business,
not in the habit of speaking to anyone.

Here is a man who loves cars. He has bought
a house on something very like a hill.
He fills his yard up with old cars. He mends things –
roofs, walls. He's biblical. He does not take thought
for the morrow, won't worry when he falls ill.
He goes swooping along on welded wings,

his children unruly, his wife losing heart.
The beautiful is what keeps them apart.

4.

The WI stall. Jams, flowers. White
hair scraped back in the draught of an open door.
The butcher's. He knows you by name. He calls
your name out. His chopping block is washed bright
by the morning sun. The solicitor
down the street. His nameplate. War memorials

with more names. Rows of Standleys, Bunns,
Myhills, Kerridges. Names on shopfronts: bold
reds, whites and blues in stock typography.
Names on labels tied with string to shotguns.
Names on electoral registers. Names in gold
in the children's section of the cemetery

by the railway cuttings. Willows, faint blue
in the afternoon, light gently whistles through.

5.

Too easy all this, like a fatal charm
intended to lull you into acquiescence.
Think karaoke. Sky. The video shop.

Broken windows. The sheer boredom. The alarm
wailing at two a.m. The police presence.
Pastoral graffiti on the bus stop.

Think back of the back of beyond 'beyond'. End
of a line. The sheer ravishing beauty
of it as it runs into the cold swell
of the North Sea, impossible to comprehend.
The harsh home truisms of geometry
that flatten to a simple parallel.

This is your otherness where the exotic
appears by a kind of homely conjuring trick.

6.

A fifteen-eighties mural. A hunting scene
runs right around the room. A trace of Rubens,
Jordaens, a touch, even, of Chinese
in the calligraphic lines. Experts clean
the powdery limewash, two PhD students
from the university, anxious to please.

A strange dome appears, out of period
somewhere near the top. Even here
there's something far flung in the code
of a different language, another God
extolling other virtues, a pioneer
morality just waiting to explode.

Flemish brickwork. Devastation. Riders
exploring hidden walls with snails and spiders.

7.

You're out at the end of the pier. It is winter.
Tall waves splutter underfoot. Gulls pirouette
and dive into dark grey. The radio is alive
with music. Its tiny voices seem to splinter
into sharp distinct consonants. You forget
the time of day. It's someone else's narrative

buzzing beneath you. New explorers come

out of the light to exploit the heart of darkness.
The world is inside out, exposed as never before.
Water and sky are a continuum.
A terrible gaiety rustles the sea like a dress
it must discard. It sweeps by just once more

then drops across the beach and remains there
in the memory, in ghosted, mangled air.

8.

How beautiful it is, this silence waiting
on salt. The disused railway lines between
wild blackberries. The faint hum of stray flies
on windowsills. Time is accelerating
down the coast road leaving behind a clean
pair of heels and a whiff of paradise.

The man with welded wings roars past, in love
with reason. His wife leaves in a freak gust,
their children flying along. Dogs race across
the walls in search of a lost treasure trove.
Gently idling, vast trucks deposit rust
in empty yards with patches of dry grass.

Broad fields out of town. The slow unravelling
of a long reel where everyone is travelling.

9.

Travelling through or ending. The damp house
beyond the library where an old woman
has been retreating for some fifty years,
and still retreats towards a dangerous
blind alley, towards a corner, where the nearest demon
might swallow her up leaving no more tears.

There are none left to shed in the overgrown
garden with its coarse weeds. It is as if
she had been sleeping a century or more,
without a retinue, simply on her own,
growing ever more querulous, ever more stiff
till rigor mortis had frozen her four score

into zero. Country aristocracy.
The dead fields at their last-gasp fantasy.

10.

A place full of old women. Hardy, courageous,
muttering to themselves and others in cafés,
engaging unwilling partners in conversation,
accosting young men, making outrageous
advances to middle-aged couples with tea-trays,
embarrassing husbands with their ostentation.

Old men in betting shops peering to check
the odds. Old men, natty in white, creaking
over bowls, with Beryl Cook elegance.
Old men tottering, sticking out a neck
at the neighbour while the latter is speaking.
Old men in the church hall learning to dance.

The old in their gerontopolis. At home
in sheltered housing, under the pleasure dome.

11.

How many times do I have to say the word: End!
and still not end. You can't go further than
the sea, not on a motorway. And what
are you doing here, yes, you and your friend
from Morocco, Uganda, St. Kitts or Pakistan?
Whatever has brought you to this far, flat

kingdom with its glum farmers? Surely you
don't think this is America where dreams
are the given, where you swear allegiance
to a new self? Have you somehow fallen through
the net of the world to be lost among reams
of legislature in these alien regions?

Homing. We are homing to the sea. Back
where we never were, at the end of the track.

12.

On a high-cloud day, you could drown in sky
round here. You see the gentle swaying
of leaves along a wall. Something under
the water, under the sky-light, in the dry
cabin under the ocean is quietly playing
a music of muted bells in soft thunder.

It is eating you away until you've gone,
like the spider scurrying up its own spit
back to its natural centre in the dark.
And the sky remains enormous. Someone
is watching the house-martin, the blue tit,
the tiny insects making their tiny mark

in the grass, and the small rain that falls far
across the field as on a distant star.

*George Szirtes (1948-*

## Out to the Fen

Suddenly, the shattered hedges, ancient copses,
our huge ruined villages, give way as
dimpled fields tilt to the Fen
and the treeless otherworld begins.

A farmer slices a vast parched field to a desert of stalks
in acres of dust and haze. Blueflies thrum
unperturbed, by a verdant ditch straight
as a Midwestern state highway, vanishing both ways

into hardly a ridge: a slope that stretches
and loops for hundreds of miles to the same sea.
Along its lip, behind dykes, the low farms and
hardened cottages stare across the flats.

It's like a coast, but what might be sea
is a sea of overstretched meadows, fresh cream wheat
nodding like so many donkeys,
dotted with clumps of poppies,

and the elders have flowered. We snip
the heads by dusk, in a silence of ditch noise
and birdsong, for cordial and fritters,
sometime later, then scatter

hares in the headlamps, and thud through clumps
of skitting gnats as distant lights
blink to let us know buildings are
over there, people are over there, and now

it's time to go.

*Rory Waterman (1981-*

## Tom Grix is Dead

Tom Grix is dead and his meadow sold, the man who
so soft spoken that the parish meetings strained to hear,
walked, as he said he realised, the whole village length
with a woman ghost.

All day my brow has ached with unshed tears.
I shed them now.
I saw our house, the russet apple tree is tall at last,
the fruit thick on it, as yet unpicked.

Oh and as I drove towards Oxnead bridge,
the sun broke silver
astonished as if the fields were full of angels,
swans and horses, warriors; another
northern winter coming on.

I called to say a new thing, something, I forgot what;
your house is empty. Tom Grix is dead
you know, I guess you know.
I have been away, changing my skin again.

We were married, you and I were married, well
that was years ago.
Odd, I grieve now:
I am learning grief.
I saw a flock of larks and
there were plovers standing in the green corn.

It was a woman ghost he saw.
He said he spoke to her and she said nothing but
they walked on and then he realised
and she was gone.

*Michael Mackmin (1941-*

## Norfolk

Those who don't know you call you 'dull and flat' –
as if dismissing a wide open face
dimpled with secret pleasures, just like that.
But I who love each wrinkle of the place –
the little towns, the vast unhurried skies,
the strong blunt Saxon tower on every 'hill',
the scathing wind that cuts men down to size,
find you the source of quiet moments still.
Yes, slow to change. Slow certainly of speech –
those back-door chats that like a minor maze
of roads get nowhere, seem forever to reach,
then with a turn of phrase or flowers surprise.
Plain-featured country woman, I have come
to call you beautiful. Take me home.

*Keith Chandler (1945-*

## Devotional for the Acle Straight

Farmland passes on the horizon, the soft steam of a sugar beet factory hangs above the flatland and seems to move at the pace of the coach. Orange curtains hang against the snow, the purple of the fields and the frozen puddles of water that I can imagine my dead dad's ghost breaking with his walking stick.

Worldly things seem so brittle, so precarious: the television masts, the fleet of white hire vans surrounded by floodlights, the two-carriage train high on the bank. We pass single drivers going the other way, the coach driver catching one last look at them in his side mirrors.

Behind us, Great Yarmouth is lighting its lights against the coming tides.

*Andrew McDonnell (1977-*

## Hephaestus in Norfolk

*And all their lifted fingers burned*

John Masefield

I walked through fields of wheat, then fields of mustard
clenched like the ear of some sleeper
who is just about to wake, who has in fact woken
but is, for whatever reason, unable or unwilling to move
This is all a paraphrase, a voice whispered
but when I asked 'of what?,' all I heard was the sky's
low and level drone, that is not about grief
that does not make incisions in the bodies of children
interred, temporarily (as we hope), in the district hospital

In the second part of this poem, I approached
the disused farmhouse, rubbish radiating from it
like spokes from a wheel, I laid first one finger, then two
against the broken latch of the garden gate
beneath me the farm lane was crushed brick, mortar
still clinging to some joints, no idea where it came from

There is no third part to this poem; I left that place

In the myth of Hephaestus, as played by the rabbits
of Edingthorpe, there is a chorus
that imitates the sounds of the hammer, the tongs
in the voices of rabbits, which are rarely used
around men, unless the life of a rabbit is in immediate
danger. I stood in the fog, watching myths
cancel one another out, over and over again, I asked

for a complete and final tally of myths
I wanted a photograph of myth's shriveled foot

I offered my apprentice as a guide to blinded Orion
Don't worry, you'll come back soon, I told him
this was not the first of my lies
broad low tone of East Anglian sky, I am listening

It is true, I wept when informed of language
and when language bore other language, I wept again

beside the mustard fields, in Norfolk in May

snapped violin of the town dormant on the horizon
pulling my tanned and stitched skins
more tightly around my approximate body
while pollen settled, inquisitive, in my brow and beard

I asked the rabbits, do you know any other plays
They scattered into the fields, into the ruined farmhouse
That's two, then, I noted
the play of presence, and then the play of dispersal
in which I am the only remaining witness
I, and the wheat and the mustard, and the scouring sky

*G. C. Waldrep (1968-*

## Near Walsingham

Springs rise where saints have prayed,
Tradition says;
And tells of rivulets and wells
Conceived of rumoured deities.

But streams would have obeyed
No peremptory hand.
Where water has already blessed the land
Saints choose to pray.

Gods walk when glint and spade
Strike, as it brims,
A buried watercourse. One dreams
A cryptic meaning for the source:

Meaning which haunts the shade
That falls by bridge and ford,
Lodged in the thought and speech that harken toward
The interminable

Tale given and not made
Or understood,
Which haunts the place. What we might say
Of what it tells would speak of God.

*Clive Wilmer (1945-*

# ACKNOWLEDGEMENTS

Every effort has been made to contact the copyright holders of the poems that comprise this collection. In the case of uncredited or improperly credited reproduction of copyrighted material, the copyright holder is encouraged to contact the publisher so that appropriate arrangements may be made. The editor and publisher would like to make the following acknowledgements for permission to reproduce copyrighted material:

Joel Allegretti: 'Mother Julian, from Her Cell at Norwich' appears in *Father Silicon* (The Poet's Press, 2006) and is reproduced by kind permission of the author.

Moniza Alvi: 'Rural Scene' from *Split World: Poems 1990-2005* (Bloodaxe Books, 2005) is reproduced by kind permission of the author.

Mona Arshi: 'Ghazal: Cley' was published online in the *Shifting Lines* multimedia installation www.mutiny.org.uk/shifting-lines created as part of the UEA's Arts Council-funded project 'Future and Form' (2020-21) and is reprinted by kind permission of the author.

George Barker: 'Morning in Norfolk', 'At Thurgarton Church' and 'A Friend's Escape from Drowning Off the Norfolk Coast' appear in *Collected Poems* (Faber and Faber, 1987) and are reprinted by permission of Raffaella Barker.

Joan Barton: 'Thoughts on Happisburgh' appears in *A House Under Old Sarum: New and Selected Poems* (Peterloo, 1981) and is reprinted by permission of the University of Hull.

John Betjeman: 'Norfolk' and 'East Anglian Bathe' appear in *Collected Poems* (John Murray, 2006) © The Estate of John Betjeman and are reproduced with permission of Hodder and Stoughton Ltd through PLSclear. 'What would you be, you wide East Anglian sky....' was first broadcast as part of the BBC's *A Passion for Churches* (1974). It appears in *Betjeman's England*, ed. Stephen Games (John Murray, 2009) and is reproduced with permission of Hodder and Stoughton Ltd through PLSclear.

Charles Bennett: 'Salthouse' appears in *Evenlode* (Oversteps, 2013) and is reprinted by kind permission of the author.

Edwin Brock: 'The Sea, The Sea', 'Tas in March', 'Morston Marshes' and 'Reedham Marshes' appear in *Five Ways to Kill a Man: New and Selected Poems* (Enitharmon Press, 1990) and are reproduced by permission of David Higham Associates. 'Morston Marshes' appears in *And Another Thing* (Enitharmon Press, 1999) and is reproduced by permission of David Higham Associates.

Victoria Adukwei Bulley: 'On Tombland, or Empty Space' was written for the *Wandering Words* walking trail https://nationalcentreforwriting.org.uk/wandering-words/, sponsored by the National Centre for Writing, Norwich, and is reprinted by kind permission of the author.

Sue Burge: 'A Peregrine Falcon on Norwich Cathedral Suffers Delusions of Grandeur' first appeared in *Best of British: An Anthology of Poems about Great Britain*, ed. Jill Munro and Sarah Miles (Paper Swans Press, 2017) and is reprinted by kind permission of the author.

David Callin: 'Snettisham' is reprinted by kind permission of the author. The poem previously appeared in *Envoi*.

Anthony Vahni Capildeo: 'Monolithicity' appears in *Utter* (Peepal Tree Press, 2013) and is reprinted by kind permission of the author.

Glen Cavaliero: 'The Church at Salle', 'St Mary the Less' and 'The Spring at Swanton Morley' appear in *The Flash of Weathercocks: New and Collected Poems* (Matador, 2016) and are reprinted by kind permission of St Catharine's College, University of Cambridge.

Keith Chandler: 'Kett's Rebellion' and 'Norfolk' originally appeared in *Kett's Rebellion and Other Poems* (Carcanet, 1980) and are reprinted by kind permission of the author.

Frances Cornford: 'The Coast: Norfolk' from *Collected Poems* (Cresset Press, 1954) is reproduced with the permission of the trustees of the Frances Crofts Cornford Will Trust.

Kevin Crossley-Holland: 'Here at the Tide's Turning' appears in *Poems from East Anglia* (Enitharmon, 1997) and is reprinted by permission of Enitharmon Press.

R. N. Currey: 'Kings Lynn' appears in *Collected Poems* (James Currey Ltd, 2001) and is reprinted by kind permission of Boydell and Brewer Ltd.

Dick Davis: 'Near Coltishall' and 'On an Etching by J. S. Cotman' appear in *Love in Another Language: Collected Poems and Selected Translations* (Carcanet, 2017) and are reproduced by permission of Carcanet. They originally appeared in *The Covenant: Poems 1979-1983* (Anvil Press Poetry, 1984).

Sally Festing: 'Sea Wall, Overy Staithe' is reprinted by kind permission of the author. The poem previously appeared in *Doors Opening* (2016), published by

Oversteps Books, and in *Between the Land and the Sea: A Community Anthology*, edited by Kevin Crossley-Holland.

Martin Figura: 'Norwich, Midnight' appears by kind permission of the author. The poem previously appeared in *City Stories, Norwich.*

John Gallas: 'Boulders on Hunstanton Beach' appears in *Practical Anarchy* (Carcanet, 1989) and is reproduced by permission of Carcanet Press. 'Sunrise on Brancaster Beach' appears in *Fresh Air and the Story of Molecule* (Carcanet, 2012) and is reproduced by permission of Carcanet Press.

Caroline Gilfillan: 'Oxnead Walk', 'The Painter of the Angels' and 'Walking with a Poet at Overy Staithe' appear by kind permission of the author. 'Walking with a Poet at Burnham Overy Staithe' was first published in *Poet in Boots* (The Brewster Press). 'Oxnead Walk' was published in *Another Country* (Cockleshell Press). 'The Painter of the Angels' was written as a commission for Art Alive.

John Golding: 'Whincover' is printed by kind permission of the author.

John Greening: 'At Swaffham, 24th July 2020' © John Greening is published by permission of the author. 'Carter At Swaffham' © John Greening appears in *The Interpretation of Owls: Selected Poems*, 1977-2022, ed. Kevin Gardner (Baylor University Press, 2023) and is reprinted by permission of the author. 'Woden' appears in *The Silence* (Carcanet, 2019) and is reproduced by permission of Carcanet Press.

Matt Haw: 'Parking at Winterton' and 'Corpse Light Footage at Strumpshaw Fen' are reprinted by kind permission of the author. 'Corpse Light Footage at Strumshaw Fen' originally appeared in *Boudicca* (2022) published by Templar Poetry.

Andrea Holland: 'Brecks', 'Tottington: Reredos' and 'Dummy Aerodrome' appear by kind permission of the author. They are reprinted by permission of Gatehouse Press and originally appeared in *Broadcasting* (2013).

Matt Howard: 'Stand in Late May' is reprinted by kind permission of the author. The poem previously appeared in *The Rialto*.

Helen Ivory: 'Thorns: Ironmonger, Tool Merchants, Garden & Home serving Norwich since 1835' was first published by the BBC as an audio recording https://www.bbc.co.uk/programmes/p047pwqm/clips. It appeared in the anthology *Places of Poetry: Mapping the Nation in Verse*, ed. Andrew McRae (Oneworld Publications, 2020) and is reprinted by kind permission of the author.

Robert Lowell: 'Our Lady of Walsingham' from Lord Weary's Castle by Robert Lowell. *Lord Weary's Castle* copyright 1946, 1944 by Robert Lowell. Copyright renewed 1974 by Robert Lowell. Used by permission of HarperCollins Publishers.

George MacBeth: 'Yuletide in Norfolk' from *Poems from Oby* by George MacBeth: copyright George MacBeth, 1982. Reproduced by permission of Shiel Land Associates Ltd.

Michael Mackmin: 'Lammas' and 'Tom Grix is Dead' are reprinted by kind permission of the author. Both poems previously appeared in *And (Poems 1970-2017)*.

Louis MacNeice: extract of 'Canto XVI' from *Autumn Sequel* (1954) appears in *Collected Poems* (Faber and Faber, 2016) and is reprinted by permission of David Higham Associates.

Derek Mahon: 'September in Gt. Yarmouth' appears in *The Poems: 1961-2020* (Gallery Press, 2021) and is reprinted by kind permission of the Estate of Derek Mahon and The Gallery Press, Loughcrew, Oldcastle, County Meath, Ireland.

Andrew McDonnell: 'Welney', 'George Harvey-Bone' and 'Devotional for the Acle Straight' are reprinted by kind permission of the author. 'Welney' originally appeared in *The Somnabulist Cookbook* (2019) and is reprinted by permission of Salt Publishing. 'George Harvey-Bone' previously appeared on the *Literary Norfolk* website.

Revd. Ali Miller: 'On Margery Kempe' and 'Mother Julian's Cat' are printed by kind permission of the author.

Ron Nevett: 'On Norwich Castle', 'On Anglia Square', 'On Caistor St Edmund', 'On *The Rings of Saturn*' and 'On Crome's *Norwich River: Afternoon*' are taken from the forthcoming collection *Norwich Sonnets* and are reproduced by kind permission of the author.

Michael O'Neill: 'Norfolk' from *Wheel* (Arc Publications, 2008) is reproduced by kind permission of the Estate of Michael O'Neill.

Hyam Plutzik: 'On the Runway at Shipdham Airfield' and 'Bomber Base' appear in *The Collected Poems* (BOA Editions, 1987) and are reprinted by permission of Deborah Plutzik Briggs and Edward J. Moran.

John Press: 'Narborough Church' and 'Salthouse, Norfolk' appear in *Guy Fawkes Night and Other Poems* (Oxford University Press, 1959) and are reprinted by kind permission of Judith Press.

Michael Riviere: 'Felbrigg' and 'On Lady Katharine Paston's Tomb at Oxnead' appear in *Selected Poems* (Mandeville Press, 1984) and are reprinted by kind permission of William Rivière.

Peter Scupham: 'Winter Farmhouse' appears in *Invitation to View* (Carcanet, 2022) and is reproduced by permission of Carcanet Press.

Fred Sedgwick: 'On William Cowper' is printed by kind permission of the author. It first appeared in his collection *The Living Daylights* (Headland 1986).

Cameron Self: 'The Brecks', 'River', 'Invocation', 'Happisburgh Haiku' and 'On the Norwich Ring Road' are reprinted by kind permission of the author. 'River', 'Invocation' and 'On the Norwich Ring Road' previously appeared in *Gedney Drove End* (2010). 'Happisburgh Haiku' previously appeared in *Happisburgh Hundred* – a collaboration with the photographer Stephen Hyatt-Cross.

Henry Skipper: 'Thar wus a young bor from Frettenham' and 'That Thar Thorpe Rail Dissarster (1874)' are reprinted by kind permission of the author, bor.

Keith Skipper: 'There was an old maid from Sea Palling' reprinted by kind permission of the author. The limerick previously appeared in *Keith Skipper's Bumper Book of Norfolk Squit*.

Stevie Smith: 'The Old Sweet Dove of Wiveton' from *ALL THE POEMS*, copyright © 1937, 1938, 1942, 1950, 1957, 1962, 1966, 1971, 1972 by Stevie Smith. Copyright © 2016 by the Estate of James MacGibbon. Copyright © 2015 by Will May. Reprinted by permission of New Directions Publishing Corp. 'The Old Sweet Dove of Wiveton' appears in *The Collected Poems and Drawings of Stevie Smith* (Faber and Faber, 2018) and is reprinted by permission of Faber and Faber Ltd.

George Szirtes: 'Backwaters: Norfolk Fields' appears in *New and Collected Poems* (Bloodaxe Books, 2008) and is reproduced with permission of Bloodaxe Books. 'This is the House the Word Built' was commissioned to celebrate the ceremonial ground-breaking of the National Centre for Writing at Dragon Hall, Norwich, and is reprinted by kind permission of the author.

Anthony Thwaite: 'Eccles' and 'Gone' appear in *Collected Poems* (Enitharmon Press, 2007) and are reprinted by kind permission of Ann Thwaite.

G.C. Waldrep: 'North Walsham' and 'Hephaestus in Norfolk' appear in the collection *The Earliest Witnesses*, published in the United States by Tupelo Press. Copyright © 2021 by G.C. Waldrep. Reprinted by permission of Tupelo Press. 'North Walsham' and 'Hephaestus in Norfolk' appear in The Earliest Witnesses (Carcanet, 2013) and are reproduced by permission of Carcanet Press.

Rory Waterman: 'Out To the Fen' and 'Broadland' appear in *Tonight the Summer's Over* (Carcanet, 2013) and are reproduced by permission of Carcanet Press. 'Losers; Winners' appears in *Sweet Nothings* (Carcanet, 2020) and is reproduced by permission of Carcanet Press.

Francis Webb: 'Bells of St Peter Mancroft', 'Gale Force' and 'Derelict Church' appear by kind permission of Therese Nelson and Maria Meere and the University of Western Australia Publishing.

Julia Webb: 'Yare Song' and 'Thetford Forest' are reprinted by kind permission of the author. Both poems previously appeared in *Bird Sisters* (Nine Arches Press, 2016).

Heidi Williamson: 'Hopton on Sea', and 'Shoe, 1979' from *Electric Shadow* (Bloodaxe Books, 2011) are reproduced with permission of Bloodaxe Books. 'Dimensional stability' from *The Print Museum* (Bloodaxe Books, 2016) is reproduced with permission of Bloodaxe Books.

Clive Wilmer: 'Near Walsingham' and 'To Paint a Salt Marsh' appear in *New and Collected Poems* (Carcanet, 2012) and are reproduced by permission of Carcanet Press. 'Near Walsingham' originally appeared in *Devotions* (Carcanet, 1982). 'To Paint a Salt Marsh' originally appeared in *Of Earthly Paradise* (Carcanet, 1992).

Cat Woodward: 'Norwich Cathedral' and 'Flint' are reprinted by kind permission of the author. Both poems will appear in her forthcoming collection *Strange Shape* published by Gatehouse.

Kit Wright: 'On a Rood-Screen in Worstead, Norfolk' from *Ode to Didcot Power Station* (Bloodaxe Books, 2008) is reproduced with permission of Bloodaxe Books.

This project was supported in part by funding from Baylor University. The editors are deeply grateful for the research fund that provided financial assistance for copyright fees.

# NOTES

### Coast

Photograph of Happisburgh lighthouse by Stephen Hyatt-Cross.

*A Very Merry Wherry-Ferry-Voyage* by John Taylor (1578-1653). This is a section from a longer poem written by the poet to record a journey by sea that he undertook from London to York via Hull in 1622. Bad weather forced him to land at Cromer where his reception was not very friendly.

*Sea Wall, Overy Staithe* by Sally Festing. Vermuyden, who is mentioned in the poem, is Cornelius Vermuyden (1595-1677), the Dutch engineer who undertook the drainage of the Fens.

*The Sea, The Sea* by Edwin Brock. The exact location of this poem is not known but it could well be Happisburgh which is a rapidly eroding section of the Norfolk coast.

*The Mill Garden* by A.C. Swinburne is about Sidestrand Mill – which is the place where the Victorian journalist Clement Scott first stayed when he visited this part of Norfolk. Scott popularised this area of Norfolk through his articles in the *Daily Telegraph* and it became known as 'Poppyland'. The arrival of the railway in North Norfolk was also a major factor in bringing visitors to the area. The term 'Poppyland' first appeared in his poem *The Garden of Sleep* (see 'History and People'). Clement Scott also fell in love with the mill owner's 19-year-old daughter Louie Jermy – though the relationship was platonic. Louie Jermy is buried in Sidestrand churchyard.

*Eccles* by Anthony Thwaite. The village of Eccles-on-Sea was badly eroded by storms during the 16th and 17th centuries and much of it was lost to the sea. St Mary's Church finally fell into the sea in 1895 but the round tower remained a feature on the beach for many years before it, too, was finally washed away. Today this area is mainly occupied by the Bush Estate and the bungalows at North Gap.

*Happisburgh Haiku* by Cameron Self. Happisburgh is one of the fastest eroding parts of the Norfolk coast. It is predicted that within 50 years both St Mary's Church, which was rebuilt in the 15th Century, and the Hill House Inn will drop into the sea. The famous red and white striped lighthouse is also under threat.

*Whincover* by John Golding. Whincover is the name of the path that connects the A149 to the Overy Bank sea wall.

*The Old Sweet Dove of Wiveton* by Stevie Smith. Smith used to stay in a holiday home at 6 Marsh Lane, Wiveton.

*To Paint a Salt Marsh* by Clive Wilmer was inspired by Burnham Overy Staithe.

### Broads and Rivers

Photograph of Thurne Mill by Stephen Hyatt-Cross.

*Norfolk* by John Betjeman. St Peter's church at Belaugh on the River Bure inspired Betjeman's lifelong love of churches. He first encountered it on family holidays on the Broads. The title of this anthology is taken from Betjeman's poem.

*When the sea comes in at Horsey Gap* by Anon. Horsey Gap is a weak spot on the Norfolk coast. If the sea breaks through here then the whole of the northern network of the Broads is liable to be flooded with seawater. In the 1950s a concrete sea wall was built along this section of the Norfolk coast to protect it. The wall begins at Cart Gap and runs all the way to Sea Palling.

*Saturday at Wroxham* by Alan Hunter. Hunter (1922-2005) found fame as the author of the Inspector George Gently crime novels but started life as a poet. He was born in Hoveton so was very familiar with the hustle and bustle on change-over day in Wroxham. Many tourists used to arrive In Wroxham by train (via Norwich) to begin their cruising holidays on the Norfolk Broads. What most people know as Wroxham is actually Hoveton.

*Gale Force* by Francis Webb. Webb was an Australian poet who was an in-patient at the David Rice psychiatric hospital in Drayton in the 1950s. As a Catholic, he was allowed out to walk to St Walstan's church in Costessey and so would have been familiar with the River Wensum – possibly beneath the railway line on Costessey Lane or at Costessey Mill.

*River* by Cameron Self. This poem was inspired by a visit to Rainthorpe Hall near Tasburgh in the 1990s. The Tas flows through the grounds of the hall.

*Reedham Marshes* by Edwin Brock. Saltwater tides often occur on both the River Yare and the River Bure and can cause the death of freshwater fish.

*Another Song of Another Norfolker* by Arthur H. Patterson. This poem is written in the Norfolk dialect. Patterson was an early naturalist and was a big influence on Ted Ellis. Patterson lived for many years in a house-boat on Breydon Water.

*Shoe, 1979* by Heidi Williamson. The river at West

Acre is the Nar – one of Norfolk's beautiful chalk streams.

*The Broads, 1919* by Hugh Money-Coutts is an extract from a much longer verse account, written in rhyming couplets, of a wherry holiday on the Norfolk Broads undertaken shortly after the end of WW1.

*Gone* by Anthony Thwaite. Ann and Anthony Thwaite lived for many years in The Mill House at Low Tharston and Thwaite wrote a number of poems about the River Tas. The poet Edwin Brock, who also wrote about the River Tas, lived next door to them. Brock started life as a policeman before moving into advertising.

**Norwich and County Towns**

Photograph of Norwich from St James' Hill by Stephen Hyatt-Cross

*On Tombland, or Empty Space* by Victoria Adukwei Bulley. Tombland is an open area in the very heart of old Norwich. It contains a number of historic buildings including Augustine Steward House and the Maids Head Hotel, and has two gates leading to the Cathedral: Erpingham Gate and Ethelbert Gate.

*Thorns: Ironmonger, Tool Merchants, Garden & Home serving Norwich since 1835* by Helen Ivory. Thorns is a well-know, independent Norwich hardware shop that was established in 1835 and is located on the corner of Exchange Street and Lobster Lane. It is famous for its twisting corridors, staircases and uneven floors.

*On Anglia Square* by Ron Nevett. Anglia Square is a shopping centre located off Magdalen Street, built in the Brutalist style. Begun in 1966 and opened in 1970, it boasted a carpark, cinema and office block, all now closed.

*Derelict Church* by Francis Webb. The church in question is St Edmund's in Fishergate which has been redundant for many years. The church stands next to the River Wensum. Fishergate is one of the oldest parts of Norwich.

*A Peregrine Falcon on Norwich Cathedral Suffers Delusions of Grandeur* by Sue Burge. Norwich Cathedral is home to a pair of nesting peregrine falcons who use a nesting box which is attached to the side of the spire. The next box has its own video feed and most years there is also a viewing station set up in the Cathedral Close by the Hawk and Owl Trust.

*Philip Sparrow* by John Skelton. Skelton took his inspiration for this poem from a young woman called Jane Scrope whose pet sparrow was 'slain' by a cat called Gib inside Carrow Abbey. The remains of Carrow Abbey still stand today in the middle of the old Colman's factory complex next to the River Wensum. Skelton was also the vicar at St Mary's church in Diss for many years and tutor to Henry VIII.

*This is the House the Word Built* by George Szirtes. This poem was written to celebrate the ceremonial ground-breaking of the National Centre for Writing at Dragon Hall, Norwich. Dragon Hall is a 14-15th century, Grade-1 listed building which stands next to the River Wensum. It is thought to be the only trading hall in Northern Europe owned by one man.

*St Mary the Less* by Glen Cavaliero. St Mary the Less is a small, redundant church on Queens Street in Norwich. It is very hard to see because it is surrounded on four sides by buildings. In the 17th century it become the church of the Walloon community in Norwich – weavers who came to Norwich from Belgium and the Low Countries. It is normally only open to the public on Heritage Days.

*King's Lynn* by R.N. Currey. King's Lynn is one of Norfolk's best kept secrets. It contains many historic buildings and churches. The town was once affiliated to the Hanseatic League and has a very rich maritime history. The Customs House mentioned in the poem was described by Pevsner as 'one of the most perfect buildings ever built'.

*North Walsham* by G. C. Waldrep. The hotel in question is the Beechwood in North Walsham and the 'famous writer' is Agatha Christie who used to visit friends here in the 1930s before the property was converted into an hotel. Siegfried Sassoon spent childhood holidays at the Old Rectory in Edingthorpe and loved the rural setting of the church. After the horrors of WW1, he returned to the village in 1937 and wrote about it in his autobiography *The Old Century and Seven More Years* (1938).

**History and People**

Photograph by Stephen Hyatt-Cross of the statue of Julian of Norwich, by David Holgate, at the west door of Norwich Cathedral.

*Mother Julian, from Her Cell at Norwich* by Joel Allegretti. Julian's cell was originally attached to St Julian's church. The church still stands today just off Rouen Road in Norwich. It was badly damaged in an air raid during WW2 but was rebuilt using the original flints. As an anchoress, Julian would have been confined to her cell and food would have been brought to her. Her account of her visions in this cell, *Revelations of Divine Love*, was the first book written in English by a woman. It contains the famous line 'all shall be well and all manner of things shall be well'.

*On the Airfield at Shipdham* by Hyam Plutzik. Plutzik was a pilot in the American Airforce during the Second World War and was stationed at Shipdham Airfield near Dereham. He was acquainted with the novelist R.H. Mottram to whom the poem is dedicated.

*Near Coltishall* by Dick Davis. RAF Coltishall was built in 1939 and closed in 2006. It was home to Lightnings and later Jaguar aircraft. More recently, it has become the Scottow Enterprise Park.

*On The Rings of Saturn* by Ron Nevett. *The Rings of Saturn* is a prose work by the German author W.G. Sebald first published in English in 1998. It concerns a walking tour along the Suffolk coast. There is a long section in the book about Sir Thomas Browne (1605-82) – the Norwich-based physician and polymath – who wrote a number of erudite works on diverse subjects such as science, medicine, archaeology and religion. Sebald was an academic at the University of East Anglia. He died in a car crash in December 2001.

*Tom Paine* by Lord Byron. Thomas Paine, a political activist and philosopher, was born in Thetford in 1737. Paine died in the USA and the journalist and politician William Cobbett wanted to bring his bones back to England.

*Kett's Rebellion* by Keith Chandler. Robert Kett (1492-1549), a landowner from Wymondham, led a rebellion against the system of enclosures. In 1549 he camped on Mousehold Heath with 16,000 men. His uprising was eventually crushed and he was condemned to death for treason. He was hanged from the walls of Norwich Castle.

*Boudicea, an Ode* by William Cowper. Boudicea or Boudicca was the Queen of the Iceni and led an uprising against the Romans. She is particularly associated with East Anglia. Some say that she is buried in a mound at Quidenham in Norfolk.

*Norwich Cathedral* by Cat Woodward. Thomas Gooding (died c. 1600) was buried vertically inside Norwich Cathedral in order that he could spring up and be the first into heaven. There is a famous epitaph on his grave – usually known as 'The Skeleton'. This epitaph appears in the 'Rhymes, Epitaphs and Limericks' section of this anthology.

*Howard Carter at Swaffham* by John Greening. Howard Carter, the famous Egyptologist, was the youngest son of the artist Samuel John Carter and spent much of his childhood in Swaffham. Carter began life as a painter before moving into archaeology. He was greatly affected by the treasures he saw as a child inside Didlington Hall in Norfolk. He unearthed the tomb of Tutankhamun in 1922.

*On Margery Kempe* by Revd. Ali Miller. Margery Kempe (c. 1373 -1438) was a Christian mystic and author of *The Book of Margery Kempe*. She is particularly associated with the church of St Margaret in King's Lynn – the town where she was born. Margery also visited Julian of Norwich (the 'anchoress' of the second stanza).

*To William Cowper* by Fred Sedgwick. The poet William Cowper (1731-1800) is buried inside St Nicholas church in Dereham. There is a stained-glass window commemorating him. Cowper moved to Norfolk in 1795 with Mary Unwin. Mary died in 1796, leaving him distraught.

*Lines to Six-Foot Three* by George Borrow. George Borrow (1803-1881) was more famous for his semi-autobiographical novels such as *Lavengro* and *Romany Rye* but he also wrote poetry.

*On Crome's* Norwich River: Afternoon by Ron Nevett. This poem is based on the oil painting *Norwich River: Afternoon* by John Crome (1768-1821) and was written to celebrate the bicentenary of the painter's birth. The painting, of a summer boating scene on the River Wensum in Norwich, was painted c. 1812–1819, probably near New Mills at St Martin's at Oak. It is owned by the Norfolk Museums Service. In 1816 Crome wrote to his pupil James Stark that a painting should be 'one grand plan of light and shade'.

*On an Etching by J. S. Cotman* by Dick Davis. The etching in question is called *View of a Garden House on the Banks of the River Yare* and is part of the Tate Britain collection. It features a hexagonal garden house perched precariously above the River Yare with a thoughtful young man seated below it. Next to the summer house sits a crouching lion.

*Woden* by John Greening. This poem concerns the neolithic flint mines called Grime's Graves which are located in the Brecklands not far from Thetford. Flint was extracted from chalk beds at the bottom of deep shafts using antler picks. Most of the shafts were later infilled which has created a strange, pot-holed, lunar landscape.

*George Harvey-Bone* by Andrew McDonnell. Harvey-Bone was the lead character in Patrick Hamilton's novel *Hangover Square* which begins in Hunstanton.

*The Dummy Aerodrome* by Andrea Holland. During the Second World War decoy airfields were set up in parts of Norfolk and Suffolk to trick the Luftwaffe into dropping their bombs in the wrong place.

*That Thar Thorpe Rail Dissarster (1874)* by Henry Skipper. On 10th September 1874, two trains were involved in a head-on collision on a stretch of single-track line near the River Yare in Thorpe. 25 passengers died including the driver and the fireman who are both buried together in the Rosary Cemetery. The accident was caused by a series of human errors. It was the worst rail crash in Norfolk history.

*Dick Bagnall-Oakeley* by John Kett. Dick Bagnall-Oakeley (1908-1974) was a Geography teacher at Gresham's School in Holt for most of his adult life but, in his spare time, he was a keen ornithologist and an expert in the Norfolk dialect. For many years he was the president of the Norfolk Naturalists' Society and a member of the council of the Norfolk Naturalists' Trust.

*The Garden of Sleep* by Clement Scott. The term 'Poppyland' first appeared in this poem. The location of the poem was the old cliff-top cemetery at Sidestrand. The present church was rebuilt further inland in 1881 using flint from the original building, and a new octagonal tower was added.

*Mother Julian's Cat* by Revd. Ali Miller. It is assumed that Julian had a cat and a number of icons depict her with one. The *Ancrene Riwle* – a 13th century guide for anchoresses – prohibited pets in general but did allow cats.

**Rhymes, Epitaphs and Limericks**

Photograph of the tomb of Edward Rigby at Framingham Earl churchyard by Stephen Hyatt-Cross.

*He who would old England win...* by Anon. Weybourne Beach has always been a possible invasion site due to the fact that there is deep water close inshore.

*The Skeleton* by Thomas Gooding. This is a famous epitaph inside Norwich Cathedral. Gooding was buried vertically so that he would be able to spring up and be first into heaven. See Cat Woodward's poem *Norwich Cathedral* in the 'Norwich' section of this anthology.

*Not like Egyptian tyrants consecrate...* Humphry Repton (1752-1818) was a landscape designer who designed Catton, Blickling, Gunton and Sheringham parks. He is buried in Aylsham churchyard and composed his own (rather grandiose) epitaph.

*There wus a young bor from Frettenham* by Henry Skipper. More of Henry's shenanigans can be found on Twitter @olehenryskipper

**Churches and Buildings**

Photograph of St Margaret's church, Hales by Stephen Hyatt-Cross.

from *A Passion for Churches* by John Betjeman. This poem was part of the script for Betjeman's 1974 BBC documentary – an exploration of the churches and rituals of the Diocese of Norwich.

*Monolithicity* by Anthony Vahni Capildeo was written as part of a residency at St Andrew & St Peter's church, Blofield. They are grateful to the Revd. Paul Cubitt and his family for their hospitality and creative help.

*Oxnead Walk* by Caroline Gilfillan. Oxnead Hall was the home of the Paston family. Only one wing of the original hall remains but the rest has been substantially rebuilt and is used today as a wedding venue. Next to hall stands St Michael and All Angels Church – the Paston's church - which contains a statue of Lady Katharine Paston by Nicholas Stone.

*The Church at Salle* by Glen Cavaliero. Salle is considered by many to be Norfolk's finest church. Its tower can be seen for miles across the fields. There is an old story that after her execution the body of Anne Boleyn was removed by her ladies in waiting and buried secretly at Salle. The Boleyn family contributed to the building of the Salle church.

*Written Amidst the Ruins of Broomholm Priory, in Norfolk* by Henry Headley. Broomholm Priory was a Cluniac priory located at Bacton on the Norfolk coast. The priory was dissolved in 1536 and all that remains today is the gatehouse, the Chapter House and the northern transept of the priory church.

*At Thurgarton Church* by George Barker. Barker lived at Itteringham, so All Saints church at Thurgarton was quite close by. The church is redundant and is in the care of the Churches Conservation Trust.

*Holkham* by Revd. Robert Potter M.A.. Holkham Hall is an 18th Century country house near Wells constructed in the Neo-Palladian style for the 1st Earl of Leicester by the architect William Kent.

*Felbrigg* by Michael Riviere. Felbrigg Hall is a 17th Century country house near Cromer. The last owner of the hall was Robert Wyndham Ketton-Cremer who wrote a number of books about Norfolk. When he died in 1969, he had no heirs so left the estate to the National Trust. Michael Riviere (1919-1997), a scholar, soldier, poet and company director, lived for many years at Dilham Grange. He was a prisoner of war in Colditz Castle during WW2.

*The Painter of the Angels at Barton Turf* by Caroline Gilfillan was written while she was Art Alive Writer in Residence at St Mary's church, East Ruston, Norfolk. The rood screen at Barton Turf is thought by many to be second only in quality to that at Ranworth.

*The Derelict Church Tower on Sidestrand* Cliff by R.H. Mottram. Mottram was more famous for his *Spanish Farm* trilogy of novels and for being Lord Mayor of Norwich but he was also a poet. This is the same church that inspired Clement Scott's poem *The Garden of Sleep* (see the 'People and History' section).

*Winter Farmhouse* by Peter Scupham is almost certainly written about South Burlingham Hall which he renovated.

*Tottington: Reredos* by Andrea Holland. In 1942 the Ministry of Defence established a battle training area in the Brecklands near Thetford known as STANTA (Stanford Training Area). To do so, it evacuated the villages of Buckenham Tofts, Langford, Stanford, Sturston, Tottington and West Tofts. At the time, the MOD said that the villagers would be able to return after the war, but it later reneged on its promise. There is still considerable resentment in the county about this decision. The village churches remain but can only be visited with special permission from the MOD. Most of the furnishings at Tottington were removed. The rood screen and some of the benches went to Rockland St Peter, while other benches went to St Peter Hungate in Norwich. However, the reredos remains. A reredos is a panel behind the altar: sometimes painted, sometimes carved and sometimes with words as at Tottington. St Andrew's has also been fitted with a blast-proof roof to protect it from shelling in the Battle Zone. The text in italics is a quote from Lucilla Reeve, *Farming on a Battleground* (1950).

*On Lady Katharine Paston's Tomb at Oxnead* by Michael Riviere. Lady Katharine Paston died in childbirth in 1629. There is a monument to her inside St Michael and All Angels church by Nicholas Stone. She helped to collect the letters that would later give us such an insight into the life and times of the Paston family. Oxnead Hall, the home of the Pastons, has been substantially rebuilt. However, one wing from the original building does remain.

**Landscape**

Photograph of the Hundred Foot Drain at Denver Sluice by Stephen Hyatt-Cross.

*Our Lady of Walsingham* by Robert Lowell. Lowell never actually visited Walsingham but drew inspiration and phrasing from a passage in E.I Watkin's *Catholic Art and Culture* (1944).

*Morning in Norfolk* by George Barker. George Barker and his wife Elspeth Barker lived for many years at Itteringham in a cottage close to the River Bure. George and Elspeth are buried together in the churchyard at St Mary's church in the village.

*Sweet was the walk...* by William Wordsworth. Wordsworth's sister Dorothy lived for five years at Forncett St Peter Rectory and her brother visited her here in 1789 and 1790. There are a number of walks next to the River Tas which may have inspired this sonnet; this was the siblings' favourite. It may not be one of Wordsworth's finest but it is remarkable to have a Norfolk sonnet written by the famous Lakeland poet.

*Yuletide in Norfolk* by George MacBeth. MacBeth lived for a number of years at the Old Rectory in Oby. Oby is a deserted village and what's left of it that lies close to the River Thurne. Place names ending in 'by' derive from the Old Norse (meaning settlement or village) and are a legacy of Viking settlement. Flegg Island in Norfolk has many such place names e.g. Hemsby, Clippesby and Filby.

from *Piers Plowman* by William Langland. Walsingham has been a pilgrimage destination since 1061 when Richeldis de Faverches reputedly saw a vison of the Virgin Mary here. The vision instructed her to build a shrine at Walsingham, often referred to as England's Nazareth. It became the second most popular pilgrimage destination in England after Canterbury. *Piers Plowman* is a long allegorical narrative poem written in unrhymed, alliterative verse.

More information about some of the locations featured in this anthology can be found at: www.literarynorfolk.co.uk

## NOTES ON THE EDITORS

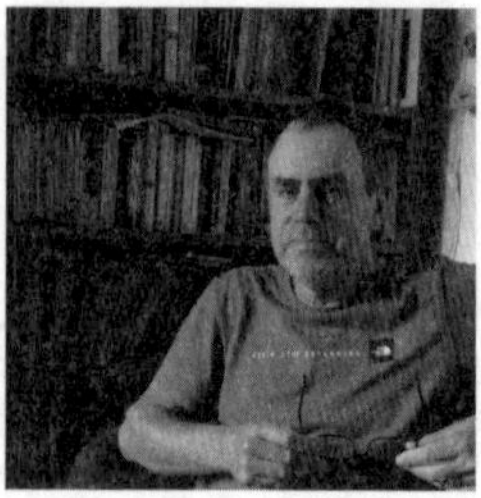

**Cameron Self** was born in Cambridge in 1962 but moved to Norfolk with his family in 1964. He completed a BA in Geography at Hull University in 1983 and an MA in Creative Writing at Lancaster University in 1985. His debut collection *Gedney Drove End* was shortlisted for the East Anglian Book Awards in 2010. His poems have appeared in the *Faber Book of Blue Verse*, *Poetry Review*, *Iron*, *The Rialto*, *Outposts*, *Poetry Now*, *Eastern Daily Press* and *City of Stories*. His photographs have appeared in various publications including *The Medieval Churches of Norwich*. He is also the author of the *Poets' Graves* and *Literary Norfolk* websites. His most recent book is *Zen and How to Get Out of Your Mind* (Waterland Books, 2022). He lives in Norwich and works at a local garden centre as a plantsman and forklift truck driver.

*Photograph by John de Robillard*

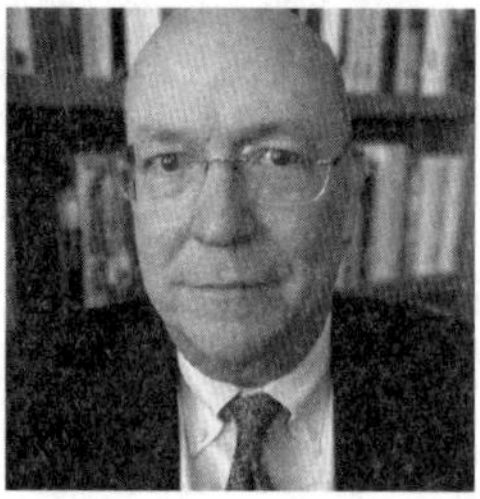

**Dr Kevin Gardner** is a professor of English literature at Baylor University in Waco, Texas. He has edited several collections of the poetry and prose of John Betjeman, including the first complete edition of *Poems in the Porch* (Continuum, 2008) and the recent gathering of Betjeman's unpublished and uncollected poems, *Harvest Bells* (Bloomsbury Continuum, 2019). He is also editor of *Building Jerusalem: Elegies on Parish Churches* (Bloomsbury Continuum, 2016), and, with co-editor John Greening, of *Hollow Palaces: An Anthology of Modern Country House Poems* (Liverpool UP, 2021). An incurable Anglophile, he has an abiding interest in the history and culture of Norfolk and its many writers.